FLORENCE AND PISA TRAVEL GUIDE 2025

TOP ATTRACTIONS, HIDDEN GEMS, FOOD AND WINE TOURS, AND EXPERT TRAVEL TIPS

NALANI BROWN

NAME

PHONE NUMBER

FLORENCE

SCAN THE QR CODE

HOW TO SCAN THE QR CODE

To access the content of the QR code (Google map)

On a smartphone:

1. Open your camera app.
2. Point it at the QR code.
3. Tap the notification or link that pops up on the screen.

If your camera doesn't support QR scanning, download a free QR code scanner app from your app store

PISA

SCAN THE QR CODE

HOW TO SCAN THE QR CODE

To access the content of the QR code (Google map)

On a smartphone:

1. Open your camera app.
2. Point it at the QR code.
3. Tap the notification or link that pops up on the screen.

If your camera doesn't support QR scanning, download a free QR code scanner app from your app store

[2025] Nalani Brown. All rights reserved.

No part of this publication may be reproduced, stored in a retrieval system, or transmitted in any form or by any means, electronic, mechanical, photocopying, recording, or otherwise, without prior written permission of the author.

The information contained in this guide is provided as a service to readers. While every effort has been made to ensure accuracy, the author and publisher make no warranties, expressed or implied.

All brand names, product names, and trademarks cited herein are the property of their respective owners.

TABLE OF CONTENTS

TABLE OF CONTENTS   5
INTRODUCTION   7
PREPARING FOR YOUR TRIP   11
    Best Times to Visit   12
    Ideal Itineraries for 3, 5, and 7 Days   16
    Visa   21
    General Safety   23
    Essential Italian Phrases for Travelers   25
GETTING THERE AND AROUND   31
    Flying into Tuscany   32
    Arriving by Train   34
    The Best Way to Split Time Between Florence and Pisa   36
    Navigating Florence   40
    Exploring Pisa   43
THE MUST SEE LANDMARKS   49
    The Florence Duomo And Climb to the Dome   50
    Uffizi Gallery   52
    Accademia Gallery   54
FLORENCE'S HIDDEN GEMS AND LOCAL SECRETS   59
    The Best Rooftop Bars for Sunset Views in Florence   60
    San Miniato al Monte   63
    Oltrarno District   65
    Secret Wine Windows   67
FOOD AND WINE GUIDE TO FLORENCE   69
    Best Pasta, Steak, and Gelato Spots in Florence   70
    Where to Find Authentic Tuscan Wine Tastings in

Florence	72
The Mercato Centrale	74
Where to Enjoy Florence's Best Happy Hours	76
DAY TRIPS FROM FLORENCE	**79**
Chianti Wine Country	80
San Gimignano	82
Lucca	83
THE BEST OF PISA	**87**
How to Climb the Leaning Tower Without Waiting in Line	88
Piazza dei Miracoli	89
The Baptistery	90
Street Art in Pisa	91
FOOD AND CULTURE IN PISA	**93**
What to Eat	93
Local Markets And Hidden Shopping Gems	96
THE BEST PHOTO SPOTS IN PISA	**99**
The Secret Viewpoint Most Tourists Miss	100
INSIDER TIPS FOR THE BEST EXPERIENCE IN PISA AND FLORENCE	**105**
How to Skip the Lines And Avoid Tourist Traps	106
Budget Travel Tips vs. Luxury Experiences	107
Local Festivals and Events Happening in 2025	109
WHERE TO STAY	**111**
Top Neighborhoods in Florence	111
Best Places to Stay in Pisa	113
Luxury vs. Budget Options in Both Cities	115
TRAVEL CHECKLIST	**117**
CONCLUSION	**125**

INTRODUCTION

Let's be honest—when most people think of Pisa, they picture that one classic photo of someone "holding up" the Leaning Tower. It's a fun tourist moment, sure, but Pisa is so much more than a leaning pile of bricks. Now, imagine hopping on a train and, in just an hour, finding yourself in Florence—the birthplace of the Renaissance, where Michelangelo, Leonardo da Vinci, and Dante once walked the same streets you're about to explore. One city is a charming medieval marvel, the other a living museum of art and culture. Together? They make the perfect Italian adventure.

This guide isn't just about sightseeing—it's about experiencing Florence and Pisa in a way that makes you feel like you belong there. You'll wander through ancient streets, sip espresso in hidden cafes, discover secret spots that most tourists miss, and eat enough pasta to make your future self jealous. So, if you're looking for an unforgettable Italian escape—one filled with history, delicious food, breathtaking views, and more gelato than should be legal—you've come to the right place.

You know that feeling when you arrive in a new city and think, "Where do I even start?" This guide is here to save you from that panic. Whether you're a first-time visitor or an Italy pro, we've packed this book with everything you need to have an amazing trip.

History Buffs – If the idea of seeing Michelangelo's David in person makes your heart race, or if you want to know why Pisa even has a leaning tower in the first place (spoiler: bad planning), this guide is for you.

Food Lovers – If you believe calories don't count on vacation, we'll take you to the best places for fresh pasta, crispy pizza, rich Chianti wine, and gelato so good it'll ruin all other ice cream for you.

Adventure Seekers – Love getting off the beaten path? We'll show you hidden viewpoints, secret wine windows, and medieval streets where you can escape the crowds.

Romantic Souls and Solo Travelers – Whether you're looking for that perfect sunset spot in Florence or a quiet corner in Pisa to watch the world go by, we've got you covered.

What Makes This Guide Different?

There are plenty of travel books out there—but let's be real: most of them are dry, generic, and make you feel like you're reading a history textbook. This one? It's fun, practical, and packed with insider secrets you won't find in your average "Top 10" list.

- **No Boring Tourist Traps** – Of course, we'll cover the must-sees, but we'll also tell you which ones are overhyped, overpriced, and better enjoyed from a distance.
- **Insider Tips and Hidden Gems** – Ever heard of the tiny medieval wine windows in Florence where you can order a drink through a hole in the wall? Or the best secret spot in Pisa for a crowd-free Leaning Tower photo? You will now.
- **Foodie-Approved Hotspots** – Not all gelato is created equal, and not all pasta is worth your time. We'll show you where the locals eat—because the best meals in Italy are never found in restaurants with menus in five languages.
- **Customizable Itineraries** – Whether you have one day or one week, we'll help you plan the perfect trip that matches your travel style—fast-paced, laid-back, or somewhere in between.
- **A Fun, Easy Read** – No complicated directions, no overwhelming lists of "must-sees." Just practical, enjoyable advice written as if a friend who's been there is giving you the inside scoop.

By the time you finish this guide, you won't just know Florence and Pisa—you'll feel like you've already been there. And when you do finally step off that train, you'll be ready to explore like a pro. So, grab your passport, loosen your belt (trust me, you'll need the extra space for all that pasta), and let's dive into the magic of Florence and Pisa.

PART 1

ESSENTIAL TRAVEL PLANNING

PREPARING FOR YOUR TRIP

Planning a trip to Florence and Pisa is exciting, but a little preparation can make your experience smoother, stress-free, and way more enjoyable. Whether you're dreaming of gazing at Michelangelo's David in Florence or striking the perfect pose with the Leaning Tower of Pisa, knowing when to visit, how long to stay, and a few essential tips will help you make the most of your adventure. These two cities are packed with history, culture, and delicious food, so getting the details right means you'll spend less time figuring things out and more time soaking it all in.

One of the biggest factors in enjoying your trip is timing. Florence and Pisa are stunning year-round, but if you want to avoid crowds and get the best weather, spring (April–June) and fall (September–October) are ideal. Summer, while beautiful, can be hot and packed with tourists, while winter offers a quieter, more relaxed atmosphere with fewer lines at museums and attractions. Choosing the right time to visit can make a huge difference in how magical (or hectic) your trip feels.

Another key question is: how many days do you need? The answer depends on how much you want to see and do. A quick 3-day itinerary will cover the highlights, while 5 or 7 days allow for a deeper dive into Florence's art scene, Pisa's hidden gems, and even a day trip into the rolling hills of Tuscany. Whether you're an art lover, a foodie, or an adventure seeker, there's a perfect itinerary for your travel style.BBefore you pack your bags, a few practical tips will ensure a smooth journey. Knowing the basics of Italian currency, safety tips, and a few essential Italian phrases can help you navigate like a pro. From understanding how to order coffee the Italian way to avoiding common tourist mistakes, we've got you covered. Now, let's dive into everything you need to know before setting off on your Florence and Pisa adventure!

Best Times to Visit

Timing your visit to Florence and Pisa can make all the difference between a magical, stress-free trip and a frustrating battle with crowds, heat, and long lines. Both cities are among the most popular destinations in Italy, meaning they attract millions of tourists every year. But don't worry—with a little planning, you can experience their beauty without feeling like you're stuck in a theme park at peak hours. Whether you're dreaming of wandering through Florence's Uffizi Gallery, admiring Michelangelo's David, or striking the perfect pose with the Leaning Tower of Pisa, knowing when to go will help you make the most of your trip. Some months offer ideal weather and fewer tourists, while others bring sky-high prices, unbearable heat, and endless queues. Let's break it all down so you can pick the perfect time to visit.

Spring and Fall: The Golden Seasons (April–June and September–October)
If you're looking for the sweet spot between good weather, smaller crowds, and a lively atmosphere, the best time to visit Florence and Pisa is in spring (April to early June) or fall (September to October). These months are a traveler's dream—warm but not scorching, lively but not overwhelming, and full of festivals, outdoor dining, and picture-perfect scenery.

In spring, flowers bloom across Tuscany, café patios come alive, and the cities are buzzing with excitement after the quiet winter months. Expect pleasant temperatures (15–25°C / 59–77°F), comfortable walking conditions, and long daylight hours for sightseeing. The Easter celebrations in Florence bring beautiful religious processions, while Pisa's Festa di San Ranieri in June lights up the city with thousands of candles along the Arno River.

Fall is equally magical—the summer crowds leave, the Tuscan countryside turns golden, and food lovers rejoice as truffle season and wine harvests begin. October, in particular, is a fantastic time to visit if you love Italian wine and food festivals. Imagine wandering through Florence's streets, wrapped in a light sweater, sipping a rich Chianti Classico while watching the sunset over the Arno River—it doesn't get much better than that!

Both seasons come with moderate tourist crowds, so while you won't have places entirely to yourself, you'll avoid the worst of the summer chaos. Just book your accommodations early, as these months are popular with savvy travelers who know they're the best times to visit.

Summer: Beautiful But Hot and Crowded (June–August)
Summer in Italy sounds like a dream, right? Sunny days, gelato on every corner, and endless outdoor dining? Well, here's the reality: Florence turns into an oven, and Pisa fills up with day-trippers like a packed subway car at rush hour. From mid-June to August, temperatures soar past 30°C (86°F), and sometimes even hit 38°C (100°F). Florence, in particular, feels even hotter than the actual temperature because of its stone-paved streets and lack of open green spaces. Pisa, while slightly cooler thanks to the breeze from the Arno River, also gets flooded with tourists, especially around the Leaning Tower and Piazza dei Miracoli.

If you must visit in summer, here are some survival tips

- **Start your day early**—hit major attractions before 10 AM to beat the crowds and heat.
- **Take a midday break**—locals escape the afternoon sun with a long lunch indoors, and you should too.

- **Visit lesser-known spots**—Florence and Pisa have plenty of hidden gems where you can escape the crowds.
- **Book everything in advance**—from museums to trains, summer lines are brutal without a pre-booked ticket.

On the bright side, summer nights in Florence and Pisa are magical. Streets light up with live music, bars and restaurants spill out into piazzas, and there's a lively, festive atmosphere. If you love nightlife and don't mind the heat, summer might still be a good option for you.

Winter: A Peaceful, Budget-Friendly Escape (November–March)

Want to avoid the crowds, save money, and enjoy a more relaxed, authentic experience? Consider visiting Florence and Pisa in winter. From November to early March, the tourist numbers drop dramatically, meaning you can walk through the Uffizi Gallery without bumping into a hundred selfie sticks, visit the Leaning Tower without waiting in line, and actually find a quiet café to enjoy your cappuccino. Hotels and flights are cheaper, making winter the most budget-friendly season for travel.

While December brings a festive holiday spirit, complete with Christmas markets and beautiful lights, January and February are the quietest months. If you don't mind cooler temperatures (5–15°C / 41–59°F) and occasional rain, winter is a fantastic time to explore.

The downsides? Days are shorter, some smaller restaurants and shops may close for the season, and outdoor sightseeing can be chilly. But if you're someone who prefers peace over perfect weather, winter in Florence and Pisa has a unique charm.

So, when should you visit Florence and Pisa? It depends on what you want out of your trip:

- **Want the best weather with moderate crowds?** → **Visit in April–June or September–October.**
- **Love the idea of summer nights and don't mind the heat?** → **July and August could work for you.**
- **Looking for the cheapest prices and quietest experience?** → **Go in winter (November–March).**

No matter when you visit, the key to avoiding crowds is simple: **get up early!** Whether it's watching the sunrise over Florence's Ponte Vecchio or snapping a photo of the Leaning Tower before the tour buses arrive, an early start can make all the difference.

Now that you know the best time to visit, let's move on to another big question: how long should you stay?

Ideal Itineraries for 3, 5, and 7 Days

Florence and Pisa are two of Italy's most fascinating destinations, but how much time do you really need to see them? The answer depends on your travel style. Do you prefer a quick highlights tour or a deep dive into art, history, and culture? Whether you have just a weekend or a full week, there's a perfect itinerary to make the most of your time.

If you're in a hurry, you can see the highlights in 3 days, but for a more relaxed, immersive experience, 5 or 7 days will let you slow down, soak in the atmosphere, and explore hidden gems. Below, you'll find three ideal itineraries based on different lengths of stay.

3 Days: A Quick but Unforgettable Experience
Perfect for First-time visitors who want to see Florence and Pisa top sights in a short time. If you only have three days, focus on the absolute must-sees. This itinerary covers the biggest highlights, ensuring you leave with incredible memories (and great photos!).

Day 1: Florence – The Heart of the Renaissance
- Morning: Start at Piazza del Duomo – climb Brunelleschi's Dome for breathtaking city views.
- Midday: Visit the Uffizi Gallery to admire works by Botticelli, Leonardo da Vinci, and Michelangelo.
- Afternoon: Stroll across Ponte Vecchio, grab gelato, and explore Piazza della Signoria.
- Evening: Enjoy a sunset view at Piazzale Michelangelo and dinner at a traditional trattoria.

Day 2: Florence – Art, Food & Local Life
- Morning: Visit the Accademia Gallery to see Michelangelo's David.
- Midday: Explore San Lorenzo Market and try lampredotto (a Florentine street food specialty).
- Afternoon: Discover the Oltrarno district, home to artisan workshops and hidden gems.

- Evening: Sip Tuscan wine in a cozy wine bar or catch a live music performance.

Day 3: Pisa – The Leaning Tower and More
- Morning: Take a train (1 hour) from Florence to Pisa. Head straight to Piazza dei Miracoli to see the Leaning Tower, Pisa Cathedral, and Baptistery.
- Midday: Wander through Borgo Stretto, Pisa's charming medieval streets lined with cafés and boutiques.
- Afternoon: Visit the lesser-known Knights' Square and Palazzo della Carovana.
- Evening: Return to Florence for a farewell dinner or catch a flight from Pisa.

Verdict: This fast-paced itinerary is ideal if you want to check off the big attractions. You'll get a taste of Florence's Renaissance glory and Pisa's iconic landmarks—but expect to be on the go the entire time.

5 Days: A Balanced Mix of Sights and Local Culture
Perfect for Travelers who want to explore beyond the tourist spots, enjoy local food, and take a day trip into the countryside.

Days 1 & 2: Florence's Highlights (See 3-Day Itinerary Above!)
Spent the first two days covering Florence's main sights, from the Duomo and Uffizi to Ponte Vecchio and Piazzale Michelangelo.

Day 3: Day Trip to Tuscany's Countryside
- Morning: Take a half-day trip to Chianti, Siena, or San Gimignano for wine tasting and stunning landscapes.
- Afternoon: Enjoy a Tuscan cooking class or relax at a vineyard estate.
- Evening: Return to Florence for a laid-back dinner in the San Frediano district.

Day 4: Hidden Florence – Markets And Local Gems
- Morning: Visit Basilica di Santa Croce, where Michelangelo, Galileo, and Machiavelli are buried.
- Midday: Explore the Sant'Ambrogio Market, a local foodie paradise.
- Afternoon: Tour Palazzo Pitti and Boboli Gardens for a royal experience.
- Evening: Enjoy a Florentine steak (bistecca alla Fiorentina) at a top-rated trattoria.

Day 5: Full Day in Pisa
- Morning: Travel to Pisa and visit the Leaning Tower, Cathedral, and Baptistery.
- Midday: Explore Pisa's hidden side—the Arno River promenade and Keith Haring mural.
- Afternoon: Take a scenic bike ride along Pisa's medieval walls.
- Evening: Train back to Florence or spend the night in Pisa.

Verdict: A 5-day itinerary allows you to explore at a relaxed pace while still seeing the best of Florence and Pisa. You also get to experience Tuscany's countryside, making it a well-rounded trip.

7 Days: The Ultimate Florence and Pisa Adventure
Perfect for Travelers who want a deep dive into history, art, food, and nature, with time for hidden gems and day trips.

Days 1–3: Florence's Must-Sees (See 3-Day Itinerary)
Use the first three days to check out Florence's top landmarks, museums, and neighborhoods.

Day 4: A Day in Fiesole (Escape the City)
- Morning: Take a short bus ride to Fiesole, a charming hilltop town with Etruscan ruins and stunning views of Florence.
- Afternoon: Visit the Roman amphitheater, explore Villa Medici, and hike through Tuscan olive groves.
- Evening: Have a romantic dinner with panoramic views before returning to Florence.

Day 5: Day Trip to Siena and San Gimignano
- Morning: Travel to Siena, one of Italy's most beautiful medieval cities. Visit Piazza del Campo and the stunning cathedral.
- Afternoon: Head to San Gimignano, famous for its medieval towers and award-winning gelato.
- Evening: Return to Florence for a relaxed night out.

Day 6: Discover Pisa and Lucca
- Morning: Visit Pisa's highlights (Leaning Tower, Cathedral, Baptistery).
- Midday: Take a short train to Lucca, a charming town famous for its well-preserved city walls.
- Afternoon: Rent a bike and cycle along Lucca's walls, then explore its beautiful piazzas and churches.

- Evening: Return to Florence or stay overnight in Lucca for a quieter experience.

Day 7: Final Florence Experiences
- Morning: Revisit a favorite spot or take a food tour to try more local specialties.
- Afternoon: Do some last-minute shopping at Florence's famous leather markets.
- Evening: Enjoy a farewell dinner with a view before heading home.

Verdict: A 7-day itinerary is the ultimate way to explore Florence and Pisa without rushing. You'll experience art, history, food, nature, and hidden gems—a perfect blend of sightseeing and relaxation.

Visa

Do You Need One?
Before packing your bags for the art-filled streets of Florence and the iconic Leaning Tower of Pisa, let's talk about visas—because the last thing you want is to show up at the airport and realize you can't board your flight!

If you're from the U.S., Canada, the U.K., Australia, or most of Europe, congratulations! You can enter Italy visa-free for up to 90 days under the Schengen Agreement. That's plenty of time to sip espresso in Florence, take too many photos in front of the Leaning Tower, and eat your weight in pasta.

However, if you're from a country that requires a Schengen visa, make sure to apply well in advance. The process usually involves:
- Filling out an application form
- Providing travel insurance (a minimum of €30,000 coverage is required)
- Showing proof of accommodation and financial means
- Attending an interview at the Italian consulate

Starting in 2025, travelers from visa-exempt countries (like the U.S. and Canada) will need to apply for ETIAS (European Travel Information and Authorization System) before entering the Schengen zone. It's a quick online process, but it's another thing to check off your travel to-do list!

✈ **Pro Tip: If you're planning to visit multiple Schengen countries, your visa should be issued by the country where you will spend the most time.**

Currency: Euros, ATMs, and Avoiding Rip-Offs
Italy uses the Euro (€), and you'll need it for everything from buying museum tickets to ordering gelato on a hot afternoon. While many places accept credit cards, cash is still king, especially at small trattorias, local markets, and transportation kiosks.

How to Get Euros
- ATMs (Bancomat): The best way to get euros is from ATMs, which are everywhere in Florence and Pisa. They offer better exchange rates than currency exchange offices.

- Airport Exchange Booths: They are convenient but have higher fees—use them only in emergencies.
- Credit and Debit Cards: Visa and Mastercard are widely accepted, but some places won't take American Express.

Avoiding Currency Scams And Extra Fees
1. Never exchange money at tourist-heavy areas (like near the Leaning Tower). They charge high fees.
2. Watch out for ATM fees. Use banks like BNL, Intesa Sanpaolo, or Unicredit to avoid high withdrawal charges.
3. Decline "dynamic currency conversion." If an ATM or card machine asks if you want to be charged in your home currency, say NO. Always choose euros for a better rate.

✈ **Pro Tip: Always carry €20–50 in cash, especially for small cafés, taxis, and tips. Some places still don't accept cards, no matter how modern they look.**

Safety Tips
Italy is a safe destination, but like any major tourist hub, pickpockets and scams exist. Here's how to stay safe and enjoy your trip worry-free.

General Safety

- Florence and Pisa are very safe, even at night—but stick to well-lit areas in less touristy neighborhoods.
- Emergency number in Italy is 112 (like 911). Keep it saved on your phone.
- Avoid political protests—they can get rowdy, and tourists should steer clear.

Pickpockets and Scams
- Be extra careful in crowded spots like the Uffizi Gallery, Ponte Vecchio, and Pisa's Leaning Tower area. Pickpockets love distracted tourists taking photos!
- Don't accept "friendship bracelets" or "free" trinkets from street vendors. They'll demand payment afterward.
- Watch out for fake petitions and donation scams. If someone shoves a clipboard at you, just keep walking.
- Wear a crossbody bag with a zipper instead of a backpack, which is an easy target.

Taxis and Transportation
- Taxis in Italy don't stop if you wave—you need to find a taxi stand or call one.
- Always ask for the meter to be turned on. Some drivers might try to overcharge tourists with fixed prices.
- Beware of fake taxis at airports! Official taxis have a license number and an official sign.

Health and Travel Insurance
- Bring essential medications from home. Pharmacies are common, but some meds require prescriptions.
- Get travel insurance. A small investment in health & theft coverage can save you from a big headache.

✈ Pro Tip: If you ever feel uneasy, step into a café, store, or hotel lobby—locals are friendly and will help if you need assistance.

Be Smart, Stay Safe and Enjoy the Ride.

Essential Italian Phrases for Travelers

Even though many Italians in Florence and Pisa speak English, knowing some basic Italian phrases can enhance your travel experience in ways you might not expect. Whether you're ordering the perfect espresso, finding your way through medieval streets, or chatting with a friendly shop owner, a little effort goes a long way.

Italians love their language, and even if your pronunciation isn't perfect, they'll appreciate your attempt. Plus, learning a few key phrases can help you avoid tourist scams, get better service, and even score a free dessert at a local trattoria (it happens!). So, let's get you talking like a savvy traveler.

1. Essential Greetings and Social Niceties
Starting conversations with the right greeting shows respect and warmth.

Ciao! – Hi / Bye (informal, used among friends)
Salve! – Hello (a bit more formal, good for any situation)
Buongiorno! – Good morning / Good day (use until 2 PM)
Buon pomeriggio! – Good afternoon (rarely used but good to know)
Buonasera! – Good evening (use after 5 PM)
Buonanotte! – Good night (when heading to bed)
Piacere! – Nice to meet you!
Come stai? (Informal) / **Come sta?** (Formal) – How are you?
Bene, grazie! E tu? – Good, thanks! And you?
Per favore – Please
Grazie mille! – Thanks a lot!

Di niente / Prego – You're welcome
Mi scusi – Excuse me (formal, asking for attention)
Scusa! – Sorry (casual, if you bump into someone)
Non parlo molto italiano. – I don't speak much Italian.
Parla inglese? – Do you speak English?

Pro Tip: If you want to impress, greet store owners, waiters, and taxi drivers with a polite "Buongiorno" or "Buonasera" instead of "Hello." It shows respect and can lead to friendlier service.

2. Navigating Florence and Pisa Like a Pro
Getting lost in Florence's cobblestone streets or Pisa's charming alleys is part of the adventure, but these phrases will help you find your way.

Dov'è…? – Where is…?
Dov'è il Duomo di Firenze? – Where is Florence's Cathedral?
Dov'è la Torre di Pisa? – Where is the Leaning Tower of Pisa?
Mi può aiutare? – Can you help me?
Sto cercando… – I'm looking for…
Quanto dista? – How far is it?
A sinistra – To the left
A destra – To the right
Dritto – Straight ahead
È vicino? – Is it close?
Posso avere una mappa? – Can I have a map?

Pro Tip: Many streets in Florence and Pisa don't allow cars, so be ready to walk a lot. And if you ask for directions, Italians might use hand gestures more than words.

3. Ordering Food and Drinks Like a Local
One of the best parts of traveling in Italy is the food! Whether you're at a fancy restaurant or grabbing a quick espresso, knowing these phrases makes the experience better.

Un tavolo per due, per favore. – A table for two, please.
Il menù, per favore. – The menu, please.
Cosa mi consiglia? – What do you recommend?
Vorrei… – I would like…
Un cappuccino, per favore. – A cappuccino, please.
Un bicchiere di vino rosso/bianco. – A glass of red/white wine.
Posso avere il conto? – Can I have the check?
Paghiamo insieme / separatamente. – We'll pay together / separately.
Accettate carte di credito? – Do you accept credit cards?

Pro Tip: Italians never order a cappuccino after 11 AM—it's seen as a breakfast drink. If you want milk in your coffee later in the day, go for a "caffè macchiato" (espresso with a dash of milk).

4. Shopping and Souvenirs
Looking for the perfect Italian leather bag or a handmade ceramic plate? These phrases will help you shop smarter!

Quanto costa? – How much does it cost?
Avete una taglia più grande/più piccola? – Do you have a bigger/smaller size?
Posso pagare con carta o solo contanti? – Can I pay with a card or only cash?
Mi può fare uno sconto? – Can you give me a discount?
Lo prendo! – I'll take it!
Posso provare questo? – Can I try this on?

Pro Tip: Florence is famous for leather goods—but beware of fakes! The best shops will smell like real leather and have "Made in Italy" labels.

5. Using Public Transport
Florence and Pisa have excellent train connections, but knowing a few phrases can make things smoother.

Dov'è la fermata dell'autobus? – Where is the bus stop?
Un biglietto per Pisa, per favore. – A ticket to Pisa, please.
A che ora parte il treno? – What time does the train leave?
A che ora arriva? – What time does it arrive?
Quanto costa un taxi per il centro? – How much is a taxi to the city center?
Può portarmi a questo indirizzo? – Can you take me to this address?

Pro Tip: In Florence, taxis don't stop if you wave them down—you need to call one or go to a taxi stand.

6. Emergencies and Medical Help

Hopefully, you won't need these, but it's always good to be prepared.

Aiuto! – Help!
Chiamate un dottore! – Call a doctor!
Chiamate la polizia! – Call the police!
Mi sono perso/a. – I'm lost.
C'è un ospedale vicino? – Is there a hospital nearby?
Dove si trova l'ambasciata? – Where is the embassy?

Emergency Numbers in Italy
112 – General emergency (police, ambulance, fire)
113 – Police
118 – Medical emergency

Enjoy the Italian Experience! Even if you only memorize a few of these phrases, you'll blend in better and make stronger connections with locals. Italians love passionate travelers who appreciate their culture, so don't be shy—give it a try.

AMERIGO VESPUCCI AIRPORT

SCAN THE QR CODE

HOW TO SCAN THE QR CODE

To access the content of the QR code (Google map)

On a smartphone:

1. Open your camera app.
2. Point it at the QR code.
3. Tap the notification or link that pops up on the screen.

If your camera doesn't support QR scanning, download a free QR code scanner app from your app store

GETTING THERE AND AROUND

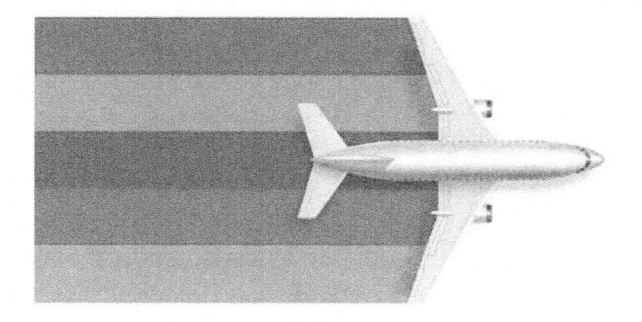

Getting to Florence and Pisa is part of the adventure, and luckily, Tuscany makes travel easy, scenic, and surprisingly stress-free—if you know what to expect. Whether you're flying in, hopping on a train, or embarking on a picturesque road trip, there are plenty of ways to reach these two legendary cities. Florence, the cradle of the Renaissance, is a major cultural hub, while Pisa, home to its world-famous Leaning Tower, is a charming medieval city that often gets overlooked beyond its most famous attraction. But don't make the mistake of rushing through—both cities have their own rhythm, and knowing how to get around will ensure you experience them at their best, without feeling like you're stuck in a tourist conveyor belt.

The good news? Florence and Pisa are only about an hour apart, making it easy to combine them in one trip. But the real question is, should you visit Pisa as a quick stop or spend the night? Many travelers treat Pisa as a day trip, arriving in the morning, taking their iconic "holding up the Leaning Tower" photo, and heading back to Florence before lunch. And yes, you can see Pisa's highlights in just a few hours. But if you take the time to dig a little deeper, you'll find a city with rich history, stunning piazzas, and lively university culture—not to mention some of the best gelato and seafood in Tuscany.

Once you arrive, getting around is part of the fun. Florence is a city meant to be explored on foot, with hidden alleyways, bustling piazzas, and world-class museums all within walking distance. But if your feet get tired, the city's tram system and taxis can help you navigate more efficiently. Pisa, on the other hand, is compact and perfect for a leisurely stroll—most major attractions are clustered around Piazza dei Miracoli, so you won't need much transportation unless you're venturing beyond the tourist hotspots.

Flying into Tuscany

Tuscany is one of Italy's most enchanting regions, home to breathtaking landscapes, historic cities, and some of the world's greatest art and architecture. Whether you're landing in Florence, Pisa, or even a nearby city, knowing the best way to get there and move around can make your trip smooth and enjoyable. Florence and Pisa are the two most popular entry points to the region, with well-connected airports, train stations, and road networks making travel easy. But choosing the right airport and transportation method can save you time, money, and stress—especially if you want to avoid unnecessary layovers, expensive taxis, or long travel times between cities.

Which Airport Should You Choose?
Tuscany has two main airports that cater to international travelers:

1. **Florence Airport (Amerigo Vespucci – FLR)**
Location: Just 5 km (3 miles) from Florence's historic center
Best for: Travelers whose main destination is Florence
Flight Options: Mostly European routes with connections via major hubs like Rome, Frankfurt, and Paris
Transport to City: The easiest way to reach Florence from the airport is the T2 tram, which runs every 5–10 minutes and takes just 15 minutes to reach the city center (€1.50 per ticket). Taxis are also available for a fixed fare of €26–€30.

Florence Airport is small but convenient, making it ideal if you're staying in the city or starting your Tuscany adventure from here. However, if you're flying from North America, Asia, or other long-haul destinations, you'll likely have to connect through another European city before arriving in Florence.

2. **Pisa International Airport (Galileo Galilei – PSA)**
Location: 1 km (0.6 miles) from Pisa's city center
Best for: Budget travelers and those visiting both Pisa and Florence

34

Flight Options: A mix of domestic, European, and international flights, often cheaper than Florence Airport
Transport to Pisa And Florence: The PisaMover train connects the airport to Pisa Centrale train station in just 5 minutes (€5 one way), and from there, you can take a train to Florence in 50–60 minutes (€9–€15).

Pisa Airport is the best option for travelers looking for more flight choices, especially budget-friendly airlines like Ryanair and EasyJet. Even if you're staying in Florence, flying into Pisa and taking a quick train ride can save money and offer more flexibility.

Other Nearby Airports, Are They Worth It?
If you can't find a direct flight to Florence or Pisa, you might consider landing at:
- **Bologna Airport (BLQ)** – A major international hub just 35 minutes from Florence by high-speed train. Often offers cheaper flights than Florence or Pisa.
- **Rome Fiumicino (FCO)** – If you don't mind a 1.5-hour train ride to Florence, Rome's main airport provides a huge range of international flights.

Arriving by Train

Tuscany's train network is one of the easiest ways to get around, especially between Florence and Pisa. The region's two main train stations are:
1. **Florence Santa Maria Novella (SMN)** – The central station in Florence, serving high-speed trains to Rome, Milan, Venice, and beyond. It's a short walk from major attractions.

2. **Pisa Centrale** – Pisa's main train station, located 20 minutes on foot from the Leaning Tower. If you're traveling from Pisa Airport, take the PisaMover train to get here quickly.

Florence–Pisa Train Route
If you're flying into Pisa and heading straight to Florence, you'll take the regional train from Pisa Centrale to Florence SMN.
Duration: 50–60 minutes
Cost: €9–€15 one way
Frequency: Trains run every 10–30 minutes

No need to book in advance—just buy a ticket at the station or online and hop on the next available train. Regional trains don't require seat reservations, so they're flexible and perfect for day trips between the two cities.

Renting a Car
A car rental is not recommended if you're only visiting Florence and Pisa, as both cities are best explored on foot, and Florence has strict ZTL (Limited Traffic Zones) where driving is restricted. However, renting a car is a fantastic idea if you want to explore Tuscany's countryside, visit charming villages like San Gimignano, Lucca, or Siena, or take a scenic drive through Chianti's vineyards.

If renting a car:
- Pick it up outside Florence's city center to avoid ZTL fines.
- Parking in Pisa is easier, but most historic areas are still pedestrian-only.

- Gas prices in Italy are higher than in the U.S., so factor that into your budget.

Taxis
- Available at both Florence and Pisa airports, but they can be expensive.
- Fixed rate €26–€30 from Florence Airport to the city center.
- Pisa taxis cost €12–€15 from the airport to the city center.
- Taxis are not commonly hailed on the street—you'll need to find a taxi stand or use an app like itTaxi or Free Now.

Buses and Trams
- Florence has an excellent tram system, with the T2 line running from the airport to the city center.
- In Pisa, buses connect the train station to Piazza dei Miracoli, where the Leaning Tower is located.
- Bus tickets must be bought before boarding from kiosks or tabacchi (tobacco shops).

The Best Way to Split Time Between Florence and Pisa

Florence and Pisa are two of Italy's most famous destinations, but deciding how much time to spend in each can be tricky. Is Pisa worth more than a quick stop? Can you see Florence in just a day? The answer depends on your travel style, interests, and schedule. Some travelers squeeze Pisa into a half-day trip, checking off the Leaning Tower before heading back to Florence, while others prefer to stay overnight to soak in the city's quieter, more authentic side after the crowds leave.

Florence, on the other hand, is packed with Renaissance treasures, stunning architecture, and world-class cuisine—so you'll need at least a couple of days to do it justice. Let's break down the best way to split your time between these two incredible cities.

The Classic Day Trip: See Pisa in a Few Hours and Stay in Florence
If your main goal is to visit the Leaning Tower of Pisa and snap a few iconic photos, a half-day trip is more than enough. Pisa's historic center is compact, and most travelers focus on Piazza dei Miracoli, home to the Leaning Tower, the Cathedral, the Baptistery, and the Camposanto (monumental cemetery).

How to Do a Pisa Day Trip from Florence
- Take an early morning train from Florence's Santa Maria Novella station to Pisa Centrale. Trains run frequently, and the journey takes about 50 minutes (€9–€15 one way).
- Walk 20 minutes or take a short bus/taxi ride to Piazza dei Miracoli.
- Spend 2–3 hours exploring the Leaning Tower, Cathedral, and Baptistery. If you plan to climb the tower, book tickets in advance to avoid long waits.
- Grab lunch at a local trattoria before heading back to Florence.

If you're short on time, this is the easiest and most efficient way to see Pisa without staying overnight. By returning to Florence in the afternoon, you'll have time to visit another museum, enjoy an aperitivo, or watch the sunset from Piazzale Michelangelo.

Who Should Choose a Day Trip to Pisa?
- First-time visitors who want to check Pisa off their bucket list but focus on Florence.
- Art and history lovers who want more time in Florence's museums.
- Travelers on a tight schedule with limited days in Tuscany.

Overnight in Pisa
While most tourists rush in and out of Pisa, staying overnight offers a completely different experience. The city feels calmer, more authentic, and even a little magical once the day-trippers leave. You'll get to see the Leaning Tower lit up at night, explore Pisa's charming streets at a leisurely pace, and even discover hidden gems beyond the main square.

What to Do with an Overnight Stay in Pisa
- Visit Piazza dei Miracoli at sunset or nighttime when it's quieter.
- Walk along the Arno River, where you'll find colorful buildings and charming cafés.
- Explore Pisa's historic center, including Borgo Stretto (a beautiful shopping street) and Piazza dei Cavalieri.
- Discover lesser-known spots, like the Keith Haring mural or the Botanical Garden of Pisa.
- Enjoy dinner at a local trattoria—Pisa has some fantastic restaurants that most tourists miss.

Pisa is also cheaper than Florence when it comes to accommodations, so if you're on a budget, staying here for a night before heading to Florence might save you money.

Who Should Stay Overnight in Pisa?
- Slow travelers who want to experience Pisa without crowds.
- Budget-conscious travelers who prefer Pisa's lower hotel prices.
- Those with extra time in Tuscany who want to see more than just the Leaning Tower.

How Many Days Should You Spend in Florence?
While Pisa is doable in a few hours, Florence deserves at least 2–3 days. It's a city bursting with Renaissance art, breathtaking architecture, and an amazing food scene, so rushing through it wouldn't do it justice.

Ideal Florence Itineraries
1 Day: A quick highlight tour—visit the Duomo, Ponte Vecchio, and the Uffizi Gallery.
2 Days: See the Accademia (David), Boboli Gardens, and Michelangelo's viewpoint.
3 Days: Explore local neighborhoods like Oltrarno, visit hidden museums, and enjoy more leisurely meals.

Florence is a city meant to be savored, and staying longer allows you to enjoy its charming streets, lively markets, and artistic treasures without feeling rushed.

Navigating Florence

Getting around Florence isn't just about moving from one attraction to the next—it's about experiencing the city. Florence is a place where every corner hides a story, every alleyway whispers secrets of the past, and even a wrong turn can lead you to the best gelato of your life. But let's be real—after a long day of exploring, your feet will start to protest, and you'll wish the Renaissance geniuses had invented escalators instead of sculptures.

So, what's the best way to get around? Florence is compact, walkable, and full of surprises, but knowing when to rely on trams, buses, or even taxis can save you time (and your legs). Let's dive into the best ways to navigate this incredible city.

Walking
The Best (and Most Rewarding) Way to See Florence
Florence was built for strolling, not speeding. In fact, the historic center is mostly pedestrianized, which means cars are banned in many areas, making it one of the most walker-friendly cities in Europe. You can walk from one side of the city center to the other in about 20 minutes, but let's be honest—you won't. Why? Because you'll get distracted. You'll turn a corner and suddenly find yourself admiring a street performer, stepping inside a charming bookshop, or stopping for "just one more" cappuccino.

Still, Florence's cobblestone streets can be tricky. They look charming in photos but are a nightmare for high heels or rolling suitcases. If you're planning to explore on foot (which you should), bring comfy shoes—trust me, your feet will thank you.

Best for: Exploring the city center, taking in the atmosphere, and discovering hidden gems.
Not great for: People with mobility issues, carrying heavy bags, or trying to rush somewhere.

Trams and Buses
When Your Feet Need a Break
Okay, so maybe you've overdone it by walking. Maybe you've spent hours staring at Botticelli's masterpieces in the Uffizi Gallery, and now your legs refuse to cooperate. This is where public transportation comes in handy.

Florence doesn't have a subway system, but it does have a small but efficient tram network. The T1 and T2 tram lines are modern, clean, and reliable. However, they don't cover the main tourist areas, so they're more useful for locals than visitors.

The T1 line connects Santa Maria Novella (the main train station) with the outskirts of Florence.

The T2 line is a lifesaver if you're coming from Florence Airport—it runs every 5–10 minutes and gets you to the city center in just 15 minutes.

Pro tip: If you're arriving by plane, skip the expensive taxis and hop on the T2 tram—it's only €1.50 and way easier than dealing with traffic.

Buses

Florence's buses, run by ATAF, are a mixed bag. They're cheap, but not always reliable. Traffic can slow them down, and let's be honest—getting on a crowded bus in the summer heat isn't exactly magical. But if you want to visit places like Fiesole (a beautiful hilltop town with stunning views of Florence), a bus is your best bet.

Bus tips
- Buy your €1.50 ticket before boarding (you can get them at newsstands, tobacco shops, or ticket machines).
- Don't forget to validate your ticket—inspectors love to hand out fines to clueless tourists.
- Buses run until around midnight, but after that, you're better off calling a taxi.

Taxis

Expensive, but Sometimes Necessary

Florence's taxis are not the cheapest option, but they can be a lifesaver in certain situations—like when you have heavy luggage or your feet have officially gone on strike. Unlike in New York or London, you can't just wave one down on the street. Instead, you have to go to a taxi stand or call one using a taxi service.

How to Get a Taxi in Florence
- Walk to a taxi stand (they're near major piazzas, train stations, and hotels).
- Call a taxi company—Taxi Firenze (055 4390) or Socota (055 4242).

- Use an app like ItTaxi, which works like Uber (since Uber doesn't operate here).

Taxi costs to know
- A short ride within the city: €10–€15
- Florence Airport to city center: Flat rate of €25
- Extra charges for luggage, late nights, or holidays

Best for: Airport transfers (if you have lots of bags), late-night rides, or when you're too exhausted to walk.
Not great for: Budget travelers—taxis add up fast!

Exploring Pisa

When most people think of Pisa, their minds immediately jump to one thing: the Leaning Tower. And while, yes, it's the main attraction (and the reason millions of visitors flock here every year), Pisa is much more than just a famous architectural accident. It's a lively, historic city with a rich medieval past, grand churches, fascinating museums, and a vibrant student culture, thanks to one of Italy's top universities, the University of Pisa.

Best of all, Pisa is compact, making it the perfect half-day destination if you're short on time. But if you can spare a full day, you'll uncover charming hidden spots, delicious local food, and an authentic side of Pisa that many tourists miss. Whether you're visiting as a quick stop from Florence or planning to stay longer, here's how to make the most of your time in this iconic Italian city.

First Stop
Pisa's most famous landmarks are concentrated in one breathtaking UNESCO-listed square, the Piazza dei Miracoli (Square of Miracles). The name alone hints at the grandeur of this place—here, you'll find four stunning monuments that define the city's architectural legacy:

1. Leaning Tower of Pisa – The world's most famous tilting landmark.
2. Pisa Cathedral (Duomo di Pisa) – A spectacular medieval church that showcases Pisan Romanesque architecture.
3. Baptistery of St. John – A circular masterpiece with a stunning dome and incredible acoustics.
4. Camposanto Monumentale – A beautiful cemetery featuring frescoes and serene cloisters.

If you're short on time, prioritize climbing the Leaning Tower and visiting the Cathedral. If you have extra time, the Baptistery is a hidden gem, especially if you catch a live demonstration of its perfect acoustics—staff members often sing a few notes inside, and the echoes create a hauntingly beautiful sound.

Pro Tip: Visit early in the morning or late in the afternoon to avoid the midday crowds, especially if you want those perfect, tourist-free photos.

Climbing the Leaning Tower
Let's be real—if you're coming to Pisa, you probably want to climb the Leaning Tower. It's a once-in-a-lifetime experience, and standing on top of a tilting building is an oddly thrilling feeling!

What to expect
- **251 steps in a spiral staircase** that leans as you go up (you might feel a little off-balance).
- Stunning panoramic views of Pisa and the Tuscan countryside from the top.
- A unique experience—there's no other place in the world quite like it.

Important Things to Know
Tickets: Around €20, and booking in advance is highly recommended.
Time slots: Only a limited number of visitors are allowed at a time.
Restrictions: Children under 8 aren't allowed to climb, and bags must be stored in lockers.
Pro Tip: If you visit later in the afternoon, you'll get a breathtaking view of the sunset from the top.

Beyond the Tower, What Else to See in Pisa?
Many visitors snap their Leaning Tower photos and leave, but Pisa has plenty of surprises waiting for those who explore a little deeper. If you have a few extra hours, consider checking out these fantastic spots:

1. Stroll Along the Arno River
Pisa isn't just about its famous square—walking along the Arno River reveals a quieter, more authentic side of the city. Colorful buildings line the water, and you'll pass historic bridges, charming streets, and lively cafés.

2. Visit Santa Maria della Spina
This tiny Gothic church perched along the Arno is one of Pisa's hidden gems. Despite its small size, it's an architectural masterpiece with intricate carvings and delicate details.

3. Explore Borgo Stretto – Pisa's Most Charming Street
If you're looking for a local experience, wander through Borgo Stretto, a picturesque street lined with shops, cafés, and historic buildings. It's a great place to grab a gelato, coffee, or souvenir (and no, it doesn't have to be a miniature Leaning Tower).

4. Try Pisa's Local Food
Pisa has some amazing food beyond the usual Italian classics. Make sure to try:
- Cecina – A crispy, delicious chickpea pancake.
- Pappa al Pomodoro – A thick tomato and bread soup, perfect for food lovers.
- Spaghetti alle Vongole – A must-try Pisan-style seafood pasta.

Pro Tip: Skip the tourist traps around Piazza dei Miracoli. Head to Trattoria da Mario or Osteria I Santi for an authentic meal at a reasonable price.

Half-Day Pisa Itinerary (Perfect If You're Short on Time)
Arrive in Pisa (Morning or Afternoon)
- From Florence, take a train (about 1 hour).
- Walk or take a short taxi ride to Piazza dei Miracoli.
- Explore the Piazza dei Miracoli (1.5–2 hours)
- Admire the Leaning Tower (and take photos!).
- Climb the Tower (if you booked in advance).

- Visit the Cathedral and Baptistery (time permitting).
- Quick Coffee Break (30 min)
- Enjoy a cappuccino at a local café.
- Walk Through Pisa's Streets (1–2 hours)
- Stroll along the Arno River and visit Santa Maria della Spina.
- Explore Borgo Stretto for shopping or a quick snack.

Lunch or Early Dinner (If You Have Time)
- Enjoy authentic Pisan food before heading back.
- Return to Florence (or Continue Exploring Tuscany!)

Should You Stay Overnight in Pisa?
If you only have half a day, you'll see the highlights—but Pisa is also a great place to stay overnight if you want to slow down and soak in the atmosphere.

Reasons to Stay Longer
- Experience Pisa without crowds – The city is quieter and more magical in the evening.
- Enjoy authentic Tuscan dining – Dinner at a local trattoria is much more relaxed than grabbing a quick lunch.
- Take your time – Explore beyond the tourist hotspots at a leisurely pace.

Final Tip: If you decide to stay the night, consider booking a hotel near the Arno River or in the historic center—you'll wake up to a much calmer and more charming Pisa than the one overrun by day-trippers.

PART 2

FLORENCE – THE RENAISSANCE CITY

THE MUST SEE LANDMARKS

Florence and Pisa are like an open-air museum, overflowing with centuries-old masterpieces, architectural wonders, and stories that shaped the world. This is the land where Michelangelo sculpted perfection, Leonardo da Vinci sketched brilliance, and Galileo redefined the universe. Every corner has a tale to tell, every building has secrets in its walls, and every street whispers the echoes of the Renaissance. Whether you're gazing up at the majestic Florence Duomo, marveling at Botticelli's Birth of Venus, or walking across a medieval bridge hiding a royal secret, you're stepping through history in its most spectacular form.

But let's be real—with so much to see, it can be overwhelming. Should you spend hours in an art gallery? Do you need to climb all 463 steps to the top of the Duomo? And what's the deal with that famous golden bridge everyone keeps talking about? This guide will help you navigate the must-see landmarks, making sure you experience the best of Florence and Pisa without museum fatigue. We'll cover the unmissable highlights, plus a few hidden gems that many tourists overlook.

And here's the best part—you don't need to be an art historian or architecture buff to appreciate these wonders. You just need curiosity, a good pair of walking shoes, and maybe a gelato in hand (because everything is better with gelato).

The Florence Duomo And Climb to the Dome

Picture this, You're standing in the heart of Florence, gazing up at one of the most iconic domes in the world, the Florence Duomo. It's massive. It's magnificent. It's a Renaissance masterpiece that has watched over the city for more than six centuries. You take a deep breath and think, Wow, that's gorgeous. But then, you hear someone say, "You know, you can climb to the top." That's when the real adventure begins.

Now, I won't sugarcoat it—this climb isn't for the faint of heart. There are 463 narrow, winding steps between you and the most breathtaking view in Florence. Some passages are so tight you might start reconsidering that extra plate of pasta you had for lunch. There are spiral staircases that seem to go on forever and low ceilings that will make you appreciate the fact that people were shorter in the 1400s. But just when you start questioning your life choices, you reach a spot where you can see the frescoes inside the dome up close—and suddenly, it's all worth it.

These frescoes? They're not just any old paintings. You're face-to-face with "The Last Judgment," a masterpiece by Giorgio Vasari and Federico Zuccari. Angels, demons, swirling colors—it's basically a giant Renaissance comic book of heaven and hell, painted across the ceiling. Some of the scenes are so intense that you might find yourself walking a little faster just to get past the creepy demon faces. But then, after a final push, you step outside… and boom. Florence stretches out beneath you in all its glory.

From the top, the view is pure magic. The red rooftops, the rolling Tuscan hills, the Arno River winding through the city—it's like you've been dropped into a postcard. You'll spot the Palazzo Vecchio standing proud, Santa Croce in the distance, and if you squint, maybe even a cozy little trattoria calling your name. You'll forget all about the 463 steps because at this moment, you're standing on top of Florence, and it feels absolutely surreal.

Tips for the Best Experience
- Book Your Tickets Early – Everyone wants to climb the Duomo, and tickets sell out fast. Grab the Brunelleschi Pass for access to the Dome, Bell Tower, Baptistery, and Museum.

- Time It Right – Early mornings are best for avoiding crowds, but sunset climbs offer jaw-dropping golden-hour views.
- Wear Comfy Shoes – Stilettos? Nope. Flip-flops? Bad idea. Those medieval staircases were not built for fashion statements.
- Check Out Giotto's Bell Tower Too – If you want another killer view (and a view of the dome itself), the bell tower is a must. Fewer people, same epic skyline.

Uffizi Gallery

If Florence is the birthplace of the Renaissance, then the Uffizi Gallery is its crown jewel. Imagine stepping into a building where every corridor, every wall, every corner is bursting with art that changed the world. This isn't just another museum visit—it's a walk through history, where you come face-to-face with the greatest masterpieces of all time. If you've ever wanted to stare into the eyes of Botticelli's Venus, stand before Michelangelo's genius, or get up close with Leonardo da Vinci's brilliance, you're in the right place.

But let's be real—the Uffizi is huge. With over 100 rooms and thousands of works, it's easy to feel like you're in an art maze designed by a very enthusiastic historian. The key to making the most of your visit? Have a game plan. You don't need to see everything (unless you secretly have the stamina of a marathon runner). Instead, focus on the showstoppers, the paintings that have inspired generations, and the hidden gems that most tourists rush past.

First stop? Botticelli's "The Birth of Venus." It's one of the most famous paintings in the world, and for good reason. Venus, goddess of love, floating on a giant seashell? Absolute masterpiece. It's the kind of artwork that stops you in your tracks, makes you forget about the crowds, and leaves you wondering how something this beautiful was created over 500 years ago. Then there's "Primavera", another Botticelli wonder, bursting with mythical figures, lush greenery, and a touch of magic.

And of course, we can't forget Leonardo da Vinci. While the Uffizi doesn't house the Mona Lisa (that's in the Louvre—sorry!), it does have some of his early works, including the mesmerizing "Annunciation." Ever wanted to see how a genius like Leonardo experimented with light, perspective, and composition? This is your chance. And then there's Michelangelo's "Doni Tondo," a circular masterpiece that showcases his bold colors, muscular figures, and a sneak peek at what's to come in the Sistine Chapel.

Tips for an Epic Uffizi Experience
- Book Tickets in Advance – The line to get in can be longer than a Renaissance novel. Save yourself the wait by booking a timed-entry ticket online.
- Go Early or Late – Mornings right when the museum opens or late afternoons are the best times to avoid the biggest crowds.
- Download an Audio Guide or Take a Tour – Trust me, a little context goes a long way. These paintings have wild backstories that make them even more fascinating.

- Don't Rush – Yes, there's a lot to see, but take your time to really soak in the art. Sometimes, the best part of visiting the Uffizi is just standing still and getting lost in the details.

Accademia Gallery

Let's be honest—most people visit the Accademia Gallery for one reason only: Michelangelo's David. And sure, he's a jaw-dropping, larger-than-life Renaissance icon, but here's the thing—there's so much more to see! While crowds gather around David, snapping endless photos of his perfectly sculpted marble muscles, there are incredible hidden treasures in the Accademia that most tourists rush right past. If you take the time to explore beyond the famous statue, you'll discover fascinating unfinished works, breathtaking paintings, and even a collection of rare musical instruments. Before you even reach David, you'll walk past four haunting, half-finished sculptures known as the "Prisoners" (or "Slaves"). These are some of Michelangelo's most fascinating works because they give you a peek into his creative process. The figures look as if they're trapped inside the marble, struggling to break free—a perfect symbol of how Michelangelo believed that every sculpture was already inside the stone, just waiting to be revealed. It's both eerie and awe-inspiring, and in some ways, these incomplete works feel even more powerful than David himself.

Renaissance Paintings
Most visitors rush straight to the sculptures, but if you venture into the side galleries, you'll find an incredible collection of Renaissance paintings that deserve just as much attention.

Works by artists like Sandro Botticelli, Domenico Ghirlandaio, and Filippino Lippi are on display, many of them showcasing the rich colors, detailed gold leafing, and dramatic storytelling that defined Florentine art. One of the best? Botticelli's "Madonna of the Sea," a stunningly delicate Virgin Mary holding baby Jesus with a background of soft, rolling waves. It's a rare sight compared to his more famous mythological works, but it's every bit as mesmerizing.

The Grand Ducal Collection of Musical Instruments
Here's a secret most people don't even realize—the Accademia isn't just about paintings and sculptures. There's an entire section dedicated to rare, centuries-old musical instruments! If you're a music lover (or just curious), don't miss the Grand Ducal Collection, which includes violins crafted by Antonio Stradivari—yes, the Stradivarius violins worth millions today! You'll also find a beautifully decorated harpsichord from the Medici family's private collection, along with early pianos and other instruments that shaped the sound of the Renaissance and Baroque periods.

The Accademia Gallery is so much more than just David. It's a chance to peek inside Michelangelo's mind, discover forgotten masterpieces, and even learn about Florence's musical history. So, while David will always be the star of the show, don't forget to explore the hidden treasures waiting just around the corner!

Ponte Vecchio
At first glance, Ponte Vecchio might look like something straight out of a fairy tale—a bridge lined with charming,

colorful shops, stretching across the Arno River like it's been plucked from a medieval painting. And in a way, it has! This isn't just any bridge—it's Florence's oldest and most famous, surviving wars, floods, and centuries of change. But what really makes Ponte Vecchio legendary isn't just its historic beauty or bustling jewelry shops—it's the secret passageway hidden above it that once belonged to Florence's most powerful family.

A Bridge Unlike Any Other
Built in the 1300s, Ponte Vecchio has been a symbol of Florence's resilience for centuries. It was one of the only bridges in the city to survive World War II, thanks to a surprising decision by Hitler himself—legend has it that he found the bridge too beautiful to destroy and instead ordered the buildings around it to be demolished. But the most striking thing about Ponte Vecchio? It's lined with shops, a rare sight for a bridge. In medieval times, it was packed with butchers, tanners, and fishmongers, their shops hanging precariously over the river as they dumped waste directly into the water (gross, right?). That all changed in 1593, when the powerful Medici family decided they wanted a cleaner, more refined atmosphere. So, they kicked out the butchers and invited goldsmiths and jewelers instead, a tradition that continues to this day.

The Hidden Passage
Now, here's where things get really interesting. Above Ponte Vecchio, hidden in plain sight, is a secret passageway that stretches nearly a kilometer from Palazzo Vecchio to the Pitti Palace. This is the Vasari Corridor, built in 1565 by order of

Cosimo I de' Medici. Why? Because the Medici family—Florence's ruling dynasty—wanted to move between their government offices and their grand palace without mingling with commoners (or worse, potential assassins). This elevated walkway allowed them to spy on their subjects while remaining completely unseen.

Today, most tourists have no idea it's there, but if you look closely, you'll spot small windows along the bridge, where the Medici once peered out without ever stepping foot among the crowds. The corridor was eventually closed to the public, but it still holds priceless artworks and stunning views over Florence. While it's not always open, catching a glimpse of this exclusive royal highway adds an extra layer of mystery to Ponte Vecchio's already fascinating history.

Tips for Visiting Ponte Vecchio Like a Pro
- Best Time to Go? Early morning or late at night, when it's less crowded. Sunset views from the bridge? Absolutely magical.
- Shopping Here? Be prepared—this is not the place for budget-friendly souvenirs. But if you're in the market for handcrafted gold jewelry, this is one of the most historic spots to buy it.
- Look Up! Most people focus on the shops, but take a moment to spot the Vasari Corridor above—you're literally standing beneath a secret royal walkway!
- Cross Over for the Best View – Want that picture-perfect shot of Ponte Vecchio? Walk to the next bridge over, Ponte Santa Trinita, for the best perspective (especially at sunset!).

LA TERRAZZA

SCAN THE QR CODE

HOW TO SCAN THE QR CODE

To access the content of the QR code (Google map)

On a smartphone:

1. Open your camera app.
2. Point it at the QR code.
3. Tap the notification or link that pops up on the screen.

If your camera doesn't support QR scanning, download a free QR code scanner app from your app store

FLORENCE'S HIDDEN GEMS AND LOCAL SECRETS

Florence is a city that dazzles at first sight—majestic cathedrals, world-famous museums, and grand piazzas that make you feel like you've stepped into a Renaissance painting. But here's the secret: the real magic of Florence isn't just in the big-name attractions. It's in the tucked-away alleys, the tiny trattorias only locals know, and the quirky traditions that tourists often miss. If you want to experience Florence like a true insider—beyond the crowds and into its soul—this is your guide. Picture yourself watching the sunset from a hidden rooftop bar, an Aperol spritz in hand as the city turns golden beneath you. Or wandering through the Oltrarno District, where artisans still craft leather goods and jewelry the old-fashioned way. Maybe you'll stumble upon one of Florence's most peculiar traditions—a tiny wine window where you can knock, order a glass, and sip like the Medici did centuries ago. And let's not forget San Miniato al Monte, a stunning hilltop church that offers the most breathtaking view of the city, minus the usual tourist crowds.

Florence has a way of revealing its best-kept secrets to those who slow down and look beyond the obvious. While the Duomo and Uffizi are must-sees, the hidden corners of the city are where you'll find its true personality—charming, a little mysterious, and filled with stories waiting to be discovered. Whether it's a cozy family-run trattoria with the best homemade pasta, a hidden passageway once used by the Medici, or a local's favorite gelato shop that puts the tourist traps to shame, this chapter is all about experiencing Florence in a way that most visitors never do. So, if you're ready to go beyond the postcard version of Florence, get ready to explore the city's best-kept secrets, one hidden gem at a time. You'll leave not just with photos, but with stories and experiences that make you feel like you truly lived in Florence, not just visited it.

The Best Rooftop Bars for Sunset Views in Florence

There's something magical about Florence at sunset. As the golden light washes over the terracotta rooftops, the city transforms into something straight out of a Renaissance dream. Now, imagine sipping a perfectly chilled Aperol Spritz or a glass of Tuscan wine, watching the Duomo glow in the evening light. That's the kind of experience you don't forget. And the best part? Florence has some incredible rooftop bars where you can soak it all in. Whether you're looking for a fancy cocktail spot, a romantic hideaway, or a lively terrace with music and good vibes, I've got you covered.

1. La Terrazza
Perched on top of the Hotel Continentale, La Terrazza is the kind of place where you feel instantly glamorous. The view? Absolutely breathtaking. You're standing right above the Arno River, with the famous Ponte Vecchio stretching out in front of you and the Florence skyline in the background. The cocktails here are as fancy as the setting—think elegant spritz variations, signature negronis, and perfectly mixed martinis. The crowd is a mix of fashionable locals and well-traveled visitors, making it the perfect place to sip, relax, and soak in the magic of Florence at golden hour. Just be sure to make a reservation—this place fills up fast!

2. SE·STO on Arno
Want a 360-degree view of Florence with a side of pure luxury? SE·STO on Arno, located at the Westin Excelsior Hotel, is the answer. This rooftop is glass-walled, giving you a completely unobstructed view of the Duomo, Palazzo Vecchio, and the rolling Tuscan hills beyond. It's perfect if you want something classy but relaxed—you can enjoy a quiet sunset moment with a fine glass of Chianti or go all out with a gourmet dinner under the stars. The best part? It never

feels too crowded, so you can actually enjoy the moment without jostling for a good spot.

3. B-Roof

B-Roof, located on top of Grand Hotel Baglioni, is one of Florence's best-kept secrets. The vibe here is a little more laid-back and intimate, making it perfect for couples or anyone who just wants to escape the tourist hustle for a while. The terrace is lined with lush greenery, and as you settle into your seat, you're greeted with a postcard-perfect view of the Duomo. The cocktails? Delicious. The service? Super friendly. If you're looking for a rooftop spot that feels exclusive but not pretentious, this is the one to check out.

4. Loggia Roof Bar

If you're in Florence with someone special, you can't miss Loggia Roof Bar. Located on top of Hotel Palazzo Guadagni, this place is pure romance. Picture yourself sitting on a rustic wooden terrace, surrounded by twinkling lights, with a glass of prosecco in hand and the sunset casting a warm glow over the city. It's got that old-world charm that makes you feel like you've stepped back in time. Bonus tip: Get here early and grab one of the swing seats—yes, actual swings where you can sip your drink and enjoy the view in the most unique way possible.

5. **Angel Roof Bar And Dining**

If you're looking for a rooftop bar with a bit more energy, Angel Roof Bar is your spot. It's part of Hotel Calimala, and while the views are still stunning, the atmosphere here is a little livelier. Expect trendy cocktails, great music, and a fun mix of people. If you're in the mood for a full dinner with a view, their food menu is fantastic—try the fresh pasta or seafood dishes while watching the sun dip behind the city's rooftops.

Pro Tips for Rooftop Sunsets in Florence
- **Go early** – The best seats fill up fast, especially at the more popular spots. Arriving 30-45 minutes before sunset guarantees you the perfect view.
- **Dress smart-casual** – Most rooftop bars in Florence have a chic but relaxed dress code. You don't need formal wear, but skip the flip-flops and hiking gear.
- **Order a classic Italian cocktail** – You can't go wrong with a Negroni, Aperol Spritz, or a refreshing Hugo (elderflower, prosecco, and mint).
- **Enjoy the moment** – Sure, take a few pictures, but don't spend the whole time staring at your phone. Watching the Florence skyline turn golden in real time is one of those travel experiences you'll never forget.

Florence is beautiful at any time of day, but seeing it from above at sunset is pure magic. So find a spot, order a drink, and watch as Florence glows beneath you—this is the kind of experience you'll remember forever.

San Miniato al Monte

If you think Florence's beauty peaks at the Duomo, think again. Just a short climb above the bustling city, away from the crowds, sits one of the most breathtaking spots in all of Florence—San Miniato al Monte. This hidden gem isn't just a church; it's an experience. A place where history, spirituality, and jaw-dropping views collide. And the best part? Most tourists don't even make it here. San Miniato al Monte isn't just another beautiful church in Florence—it's one of the oldest, dating back to the 11th century. Named after Saint Minias, a Christian martyr who, according to legend, was beheaded in Florence and then picked up his own head and walked to this very hill before collapsing. (Yes, really. Florence has a flair for the dramatic.) But eerie legends aside, the church itself is a masterpiece of Romanesque architecture, with intricate marble floors, stunning mosaics, and an interior so peaceful it feels like stepping into another world.

Here's the real reason you need to visit San Miniato al Monte: the view. Standing on the church's terrace, you get a sweeping, panoramic view of Florence—the Duomo, the Arno River, the rolling Tuscan hills in the distance. It's like a Renaissance painting come to life. And unlike Piazzale Michelangelo (which, let's be honest, is overrun with selfie sticks), San Miniato offers a quieter, more intimate experience. It's the perfect place to pause, take a deep breath, and soak in the beauty of Florence without distractions.

If you time your visit right, you might just witness something truly magical. Every evening, the monks of San Miniato al Monte perform Gregorian chants, filling the church with hauntingly beautiful melodies. It's an experience that gives you chills in the best way possible—a moment of pure serenity in the heart of Florence.

How to Get There

- **Walking**: If you're up for a scenic but slightly challenging walk, start from Ponte Vecchio and make your way up through Piazzale Michelangelo. The climb is steep, but the views make it 100% worth it.
- **By Bus**: Take bus 12 or 13 from the city center and hop off near the church for a less exhausting route.
- **By Taxi**: If you're feeling fancy (or just tired), a quick taxi ride will get you there in minutes.

Oltrarno District

If you're craving a slice of Florence that feels more authentic and less touristy, look no further than the Oltrarno district. Often referred to as "the real Florence," this charming area on the southern side of the Arno River offers a refreshing escape from the hustle and bustle of the more famous landmarks. While tourists flock to the Duomo and Uffizi, Oltrarno is where you'll find Florence's heart and soul, with its cobbled streets, hidden artisan workshops, and family-run trattorias that serve up the flavors of true Tuscan hospitality.

Oltrarno is a paradise for anyone interested in authentic craftsmanship. As you wander through the narrow lanes, you'll stumble upon shops run by skilled artisans practicing ancient traditions passed down through generations. From leather craftsmen creating bespoke bags to woodworkers carving intricate furniture, this is where you'll find works of art that aren't on display in museums—they're on sale in tiny boutiques. Want a unique souvenir? Look no further than the hand-painted pottery or custom-made jewelry, each piece telling a story of Florence's artistic heritage. Be sure to check out the famous Florentine paper shops, where you can browse through beautiful notebooks and stationery that reflect the city's vibrant creativity.

If you're a foodie (or simply someone who loves good food), Oltrarno's trattorias are a must. While the city center is home to its fair share of touristy restaurants, the local eateries in Oltrarno offer authentic Tuscan meals that will transport your taste buds straight to nonna's kitchen. Whether you're craving bistecca alla fiorentina (Florentine steak), ribollita (hearty vegetable soup), or pappardelle with wild boar, the Oltrarno trattorias know how to cook with love and tradition. Cozy, intimate settings, with just a few tables and a genuine, welcoming atmosphere, make it the perfect spot for a leisurely dinner away from the crowds. Don't forget to try a glass of Chianti—after all, you're in the heart of Tuscany

At the center of Oltrarno lies Piazza Santo Spirito, a bustling square that's perfect for people-watching, sipping an espresso, or indulging in a gelato. Surrounded by quaint cafés and restaurants, the piazza is also home to the Santo Spirito Church, a masterpiece by Brunelleschi that stands as a serene backdrop to the daily life of locals. In the evening, the square comes alive with a relaxed vibe, as both locals and travelers gather to enjoy aperitivo (Italian happy hour) or just chill with a spritz. On certain days, you can also find an open-air market here, where you can browse through antiques, vintage items, and artisan goods, making it an ideal place to soak up the culture and vibe of this historic district.

What makes Oltrarno so special isn't just its history or its crafts—it's the feeling that you're walking through a neighborhood that's lived in, where locals carry on their daily routines with a sense of pride and community. This is the Florence that gives you room to breathe, where you can explore at your own pace and really feel like you've stepped off the beaten path. Oltrarno is the perfect spot to experience Florence's local side—the Florence that isn't found in travel guides or on Instagram feeds. So the next time you visit Florence, venture beyond the famous sights and lose yourself in the charm of Oltrarno—you might just find your favorite part of the city.

Secret Wine Windows

Imagine strolling through the narrow, picturesque streets of Florence, the sun beginning to set, and you're feeling like you've stepped back in time. Suddenly, you stumble upon what seems like an ordinary, unassuming window—but wait—this isn't just any window. This, my friend, is one of Florence's secret wine windows (known as "buchette del vino"), a historical treasure that lets you sip wine like a true Medici. Yes, you read that right—sip wine through a window!

The story of Florence's wine windows goes all the way back to the 16th century, when the Medici family—the powerful rulers of Tuscany—had a unique way of enjoying their wine. In an era when Florence was a bustling center of trade, wine was abundant, and the city's wealthy elite wanted a way to enjoy their favorite local wines without the prying eyes of the public. So, they had special wine windows built into their homes and wineries. These tiny, circular or square windows were small enough to keep the elite's wine tasting hidden, yet large enough to pass a bottle or glass through to those on the street. It was their own private wine delivery service! Today, these historic windows are scattered across the Oltrarno district and beyond, often tucked away on unassuming streets or behind lush vines. Some are almost invisible, blending in with the surrounding architecture, while others are proudly restored, showcasing their historical charm. If you're on the hunt for a wine window, keep your eyes peeled as you wander through Florence's backstreets—especially in the artisan neighborhoods like Oltrarno, where local wineries and historical buildings still preserve these hidden gems.

Okay, so you've found a secret wine window. What's next? Here's where the fun begins. These days, some of Florence's best wine bars and small family-run wineries have reimagined the historic concept of the wine window by offering local wines to passersby through these charming openings. So, no need to be a Medici to enjoy: just approach the window, make a purchase, and you'll be handed a glass of superb Tuscan wine, often served with a side of warm bread and olive oil. It's a little taste of history and a sip of Tuscany all in one. Drinking wine through a secret window might sound quirky, but there's something wonderfully authentic and fun about this experience. It's a way to connect with the city's past while savoring one of Italy's greatest pleasures: wine. While you won't be able to find every window serving wine (some are private, some are just historical artifacts), there are a few spots where locals and visitors alike can enjoy a glass of vino the way the Medici might have. It's not just about drinking wine;

it's about stepping into history and sharing a secret with the city's past.

FOOD AND WINE GUIDE TO FLORENCE

From the rich, hearty pastas to the melt-in-your-mouth steaks, the food scene in Florence is a love letter to Tuscan culinary traditions. Whether you're a foodie on a mission to savor every bite or just someone looking for an unforgettable meal, this guide will make sure your time in Florence is as delicious as it is memorable. If there's one thing that defines Tuscan cuisine, it's simplicity. The best dishes don't need fancy ingredients or complex recipes. They focus on the quality of the ingredients and the skillful art of cooking them to perfection. We're talking about pasta so fresh you'll wonder if it's made just for you, steaks so tender they practically melt in your mouth, and gelato so good, you'll likely have a second (or third) scoop before you leave. But, it's not just about the food. The wine here is as rich in flavor as the landscape, with world-class vineyards that serve up perfect pours to complement every dish.

Of course, Florence is more than just iconic dishes. It's also a food lover's playground, brimming with local markets, vibrant street food stalls, and charming family-run eateries where the chefs will treat you like family. From the bustling Mercato Centrale, where you can taste fresh pasta, artisan cheeses, and cured meats, to the hidden gems scattered across the city, Florence offers a culinary adventure waiting to be explored. And don't forget about the aperitivo culture—the best way to enjoy Florence's relaxed evening vibe with an Italian cocktail and small bites.

Best Pasta, Steak, and Gelato Spots in Florence

Florence's food scene is a vibrant celebration of the flavors and traditions of Tuscany, and if there's one thing you absolutely can't miss, it's the pasta, steak, and gelato. Whether you're on a culinary pilgrimage or simply in search of your next meal, Florence offers some of the best dining experiences that will leave you craving more. So, let's dive into the ultimate foodie hotspots for these three iconic dishes.

Pasta Heaven

When it comes to pasta, Florence takes it seriously. The city is home to countless eateries that serve up homemade, handmade pasta with every possible variation. One of the absolute best spots for pasta is Trattoria ZaZa, located near the San Lorenzo Market. Known for its pappardelle al cinghiale (wild boar ragu), ZaZa's rich, tender pasta will make your taste buds dance. Another top contender is Osteria Santo Spirito, tucked away in the Oltrarno district, where you'll find pasta made fresh daily, including some unforgettable tagliatelle with truffle sauce that will transport you straight to pasta heaven. And for a true taste of traditional Tuscan pasta, Cucina Torcicoda in the heart of Florence serves up a mouthwatering pasta alla fiorentina, featuring rich, creamy Florentine sauce with homemade ravioli.

Steak

If you've come to Florence, you're in for a treat when it comes to steak. The bistecca alla fiorentina, Florence's iconic T-bone steak, is an absolute must-try. To taste the best, head to Trattoria Sostanza, a Florence institution known for serving up the juiciest, most perfectly cooked bistecca in the city. The meat is always tender and succulent, and grilled to perfection—a true representation of Tuscan cooking at its finest. Another spot where you'll get a top-notch bistecca is Osteria del Cinghiale Bianco, where you can enjoy the classic Florence steak with a side of Tuscan beans and rosemary potatoes. For a more elevated experience, check out La Giostra, a romantic and cozy restaurant where the bistecca is served with the utmost flair and accompanied by seasonal sides that pair perfectly with the smoky, charred flavors of the meat.

Gelato

No meal in Florence is complete without a stop for gelato, and let's be honest—Florence serves some of the best gelato in the world. If you want a true gelato experience, head straight to Gelateria La Carraia, where you'll find mouthwatering flavors like pistachio, chocolate hazelnut, and ricotta with fig that will have you savoring every bite. Vivoli is another Florence gem, one of the city's oldest gelaterias, serving up creamy, dense gelato with flavors that taste as though they've been crafted with the finest local ingredients. And, if you're looking for a slightly more adventurous take on gelato, Gelateria dei Neri near Santa Croce offers more unusual flavor combinations like rosemary and honey or saffron gelato that are worth a try. Trust us, these spots will have you saying, "I'll take one more scoop, please."

Florence truly shines when it comes to food, with pasta, steak, and gelato as the stars of the show. Whether you're looking to try classic Tuscan flavors or indulge in something a bit more innovative, the city offers an abundance of options to satisfy any craving. So, bring your appetite, and get ready for an unforgettable food adventure in this charming Italian city.

Where to Find Authentic Tuscan Wine Tastings in Florence

Tuscan wine is more than just a drink—it's an experience, a way to connect with centuries of winemaking tradition that stretches back to the Romans. Whether you're a seasoned wine connoisseur or just looking to learn more, Florence is full of incredible places to sip, swirl, and savor the very best of Tuscany's wine culture.

Start your journey with a visit to Le Volpi e L'Uva, a tiny gem tucked away just off Ponte Vecchio. This wine shop-cum-tasting bar offers a handpicked selection of Tuscan wines, from Chianti Classico to the rich Brunello di Montalcino. The staff is incredibly knowledgeable and will happily walk you through a personalized tasting experience, explaining the nuances of each wine and its connection to the surrounding region. Not only will you learn about the wines, but you'll also get a glimpse into the stories of the small, family-owned vineyards that produce them. It's an intimate, educational, and absolutely delicious way to kick off your wine adventure.

For a more immersive experience, head to Cantinetta Antinori, the stunning wine cellar located beneath the historic Antinori family's Florentine palace. Antinori is one of Tuscany's oldest and most prestigious wine families, with a history dating back to 1385. The cellar itself is a masterpiece of modern architecture, with glass walls that let you look into the aging chambers, where Barolo and Super Tuscans mature in quiet perfection. Here, you'll enjoy a guided wine tasting featuring their iconic wines, and the knowledgeable staff will walk you through the rich history of the Antinori family's impact on the Tuscan wine industry. The best part? You get to sample some exceptional wines paired with local cheeses and charcuterie—talk about living the Tuscan dream!

Now, if you're looking for a hands-on experience and a chance to step outside the city, book a day trip to one of Tuscany's famous vineyard estates. Fattoria di Maiano, a short drive from Florence, offers wine tastings set against a breathtaking backdrop of the Tuscan hills. Take a guided tour of the vineyards and learn the traditional methods of winemaking before enjoying a tasting session in the estate's charming rustic tasting room. The wines here are organic and reflect the true spirit of Tuscany. Afterward, you can enjoy a hearty Tuscan meal in their restaurant, where the local dishes perfectly complement the wines you've just sampled.

Last but certainly not least, for those who want an extra touch of luxury, consider booking a private wine-tasting tour with Florence Wine Tours. This company specializes in customized tours that allow you to visit some of the finest wineries in the Chianti region, all while being guided by an expert sommelier who can explain the intricacies of Tuscan wines. Whether you're interested in tasting rare Super Tuscans, exploring family-owned wineries, or learning about sustainable viticulture practices, these tours are an unforgettable experience that brings you right to the heart of Tuscany's winemaking world.

The Mercato Centrale

The Mercato Centrale in Florence is nothing short of a dream for food lovers. It's a place where the freshest ingredients, the finest local produce, and mouth-watering aromas all come together under one roof. Located in the San Lorenzo district, this bustling market has been a staple of Florence since 1874, and it's more than just a place to buy food—it's a true celebration of Italian gastronomy.

The ground floor is where you'll find a traditional market atmosphere, packed with fresh meats, cheeses, vegetables, and fruits. The vibrancy of the market comes alive here—locals haggle with friendly vendors for the best cuts of prosciutto, sample creamy buffalo mozzarella, or grab some freshly picked tomatoes. Whether you're a seasoned cook or a curious visitor, you'll find yourself wandering between stalls, discovering local ingredients you may never have seen before. It's the perfect spot to pick up something special for a homemade Italian meal or even just grab a snack on the go.

Upstairs, the modern food hall takes things to a whole new level. Imagine a variety of gourmet food stalls, each serving up a unique taste of Tuscany. From handmade pasta to freshly baked pizza, and artisanal gelato to exquisite local wines, the selection is mouthwatering. If you want to dive into authentic Tuscan dishes, this is the place to do it. You can feast on a bowl of ribollita, a hearty Tuscan soup, or indulge in a plate of bistecca alla fiorentina, Florence's famous steak. For dessert, don't miss the chance to sample a cantucci with a glass of vin santo—a local dessert wine that's a match made in heaven with these crunchy almond biscuits.

But it's not just about the food. The atmosphere at Mercato Centrale is something special. The market is always lively, with locals, tourists, and chefs alike all sharing the space. It's a place where food becomes a community experience, whether you're sitting at one of the tables with a glass of Chianti or chatting with a stall owner about their fresh truffles. And if you're really into food, there are also cooking classes and food tours available to dive deeper into the local cuisine and get some hands-on experience in the kitchen.

Where to Enjoy Florence's Best Happy Hours

In Florence, aperitivo hour isn't just a tradition – it's a way of life. This cherished pre-dinner ritual is the perfect blend of socializing, snacking, and sipping a refreshing drink. Think of it as a way to unwind after a day of exploring, where you gather with friends or fellow travelers to enjoy a drink and light bites before the main meal. The beauty of aperitivo culture is that it's all about savoring the moment, whether you're enjoying a classic Negroni, a glass of local Chianti, or an ice-cold spritz.

The best part? Aperitivo hour typically includes more than just a drink. Many bars and cafes in Florence offer a delightful spread of complimentary snacks when you order a drink. These snacks can range from olives and nuts to an extravagant spread of cheeses, cured meats, crostini, and even mini sandwiches. At some places, you'll find a buffet of pasta dishes, salads, and pizza slices, making aperitivo a meal in itself. So not only do you get to sip your favorite drink, but you also get to nibble on some delicious local fare—sometimes even enough to make a full dinner out of it!

One of the best places to dive into the aperitivo culture is the Oltrarno district, known for its laid-back vibe and quirky bars. You'll find cozy spots like La Cova offering a relaxed atmosphere and a great selection of Italian wines. If you're in the mood for something with a little more elegance, Fellini Bar is where Florence's chic crowd gathers for a refined aperitivo experience. The stylish interiors and sweeping views of the Arno River make it the perfect spot to sip a cocktail as the sun sets over the city.

For an authentic experience, don't miss the iconic Caffè Gilli, one of the oldest cafes in Florence, located in Piazza della Repubblica. Here, you'll find locals and tourists alike gathering for their aperitivo ritual. Whether you choose an expertly crafted cocktail or a glass of Prosecco, you can enjoy it alongside an elegant selection of pastries and cured meats, all while soaking in the lively atmosphere of this historic cafe. If you're after something a little more off-the-beaten-path, head to Bar La Menagère. This trendy venue blends a café, bar, and restaurant, making it a favorite spot for aperitivo lovers who also want to enjoy artfully crafted cocktails and a truly Florentine vibe.

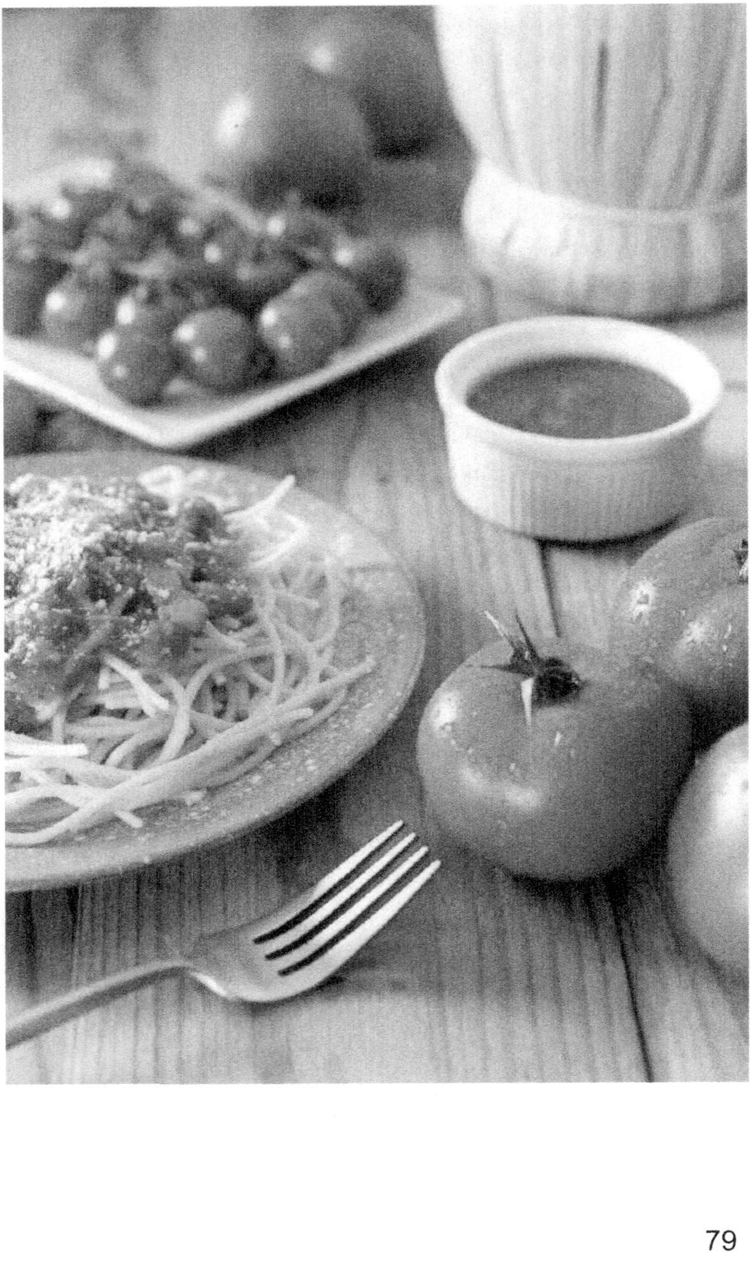

DAY TRIPS FROM FLORENCE

It was one of those mornings in Florence where everything seemed just a little extra magical. The sun was gently waking up, casting a soft glow on the cobblestone streets, and the city felt quieter than usual. After a few days of museum hopping, gelato eating, and getting lost in Florence's maze of streets, I was craving something new—something a little off the beaten path. I had heard whispers about the small towns and villages just outside the city, and I decided it was time to go check them out for myself.

So, I hopped on a train, not really knowing what to expect. As the city disappeared behind me, I felt like I was stepping into a completely different world. The view from the window was like something out of a postcard—vineyards stretching forever, tiny villages tucked in the hills, and fields dotted with olive trees. It was like Florence was the busy, vibrant city, and the countryside was the peaceful, laid-back twin. And the best part? No crowds! Just me and the open road (well, tracks, but you get the idea). The train finally stopped, and I stepped off into the fresh, countryside air. The Chianti wine region welcomed me with its lush landscape, and I wandered through one of the vineyards, taking in the sights and smells of the grapes.

I was greeted by a local winemaker who invited me to try his wine. One sip, and I understood why people rave about Tuscan wine—it was like tasting the sun, the earth, and everything in between. This wasn't just wine; it was a piece of Tuscany itself. The more I explored, the more I realized that Tuscany isn't just about Florence's famous art and architecture. It's about the quiet hills, the small villages, and the hidden gems that are waiting to be discovered. If you're ever in Florence, take a day (or two) to hop on a train and see what's waiting beyond the city. Trust me, the adventure is worth it, and you might just find your new favorite spot in all of Tuscany.

Chianti Wine Country

Chianti Wine Country is one of Tuscany's most famous regions, and for good reason. Known for its scenic beauty and world-renowned wines, this is the place to experience the essence of Tuscany. The region, located between Florence and Siena, is dotted with picturesque vineyards, charming hilltop villages, and centuries-old wineries that offer an authentic Tuscan wine experience. Whether you're a seasoned wine enthusiast or just looking to enjoy the beautiful landscape with a glass of wine in hand, Chianti won't disappoint.

Castello di Verrazzano is one of the top destinations for wine lovers in the region. Located in the heart of the Chianti Classico area, this historic winery is housed in a 16th-century castle and offers guided tours of its cellars and vineyards. As you stroll through the castle grounds, you'll learn about the history of Chianti wine-making before settling down for a tasting session. The panoramic views from the winery are stunning, making it an ideal spot to sip a glass of Chianti while enjoying the rolling hills below.

For a more intimate experience, Fattoria La Vialla is a hidden gem that offers a more personal and rustic wine tasting experience. Located just outside of Rignano sull'Arno, this organic farm produces wines, olive oils, and a variety of other local products. The vineyard's family-friendly atmosphere and commitment to sustainability make it an excellent choice for those looking to explore traditional Tuscan farming methods. Here, you can enjoy a wine tasting paired with cheeses and meats sourced from local farms while learning about the process of making organic wine.

If you're seeking a unique combination of history and wine, head to Badia a Coltibuono. This ancient abbey, dating back to the 11th century, is a fantastic place to immerse yourself in the rich history of the region while sampling some of the finest Chianti wines. The winery's history and the stunning surroundings of the vineyard offer a peaceful retreat, and their wine tasting tours are informative and engaging, making it a perfect stop for history buffs and wine enthusiasts alike.

No matter which vineyard you choose to visit, Chianti Wine Country offers an unforgettable experience. The combination of rich history, beautiful scenery, and exquisite wines makes it a must-see destination for anyone visiting Tuscany. Be sure to take your time, savor the wines, and soak in the natural beauty that surrounds you—after all, this is where some of the world's best wines are made.

San Gimignano

Often referred to as the "Medieval Manhattan" because of its skyline filled with towering medieval towers, San Gimignano is one of Tuscany's most enchanting towns. This UNESCO World Heritage Site is perched on a hilltop and is famous for its well-preserved medieval architecture. It's like stepping back in time, where narrow cobblestone streets and ancient buildings transport you to a different era. The town's towers, built by wealthy families during the 12th and 13th centuries, rise high above the surrounding Tuscan countryside, giving San Gimignano its distinctive skyline.

The town's medieval charm is evident at every turn, from the well-preserved walls surrounding the old town to the gorgeous squares and churches dotted around. The most famous of these is Piazza del Duomo, where you'll find the town's cathedral, Collegiata di San Gimignano. Inside, you can admire breathtaking frescoes that tell the stories of the Old and New Testaments. For a more panoramic view, head to Piazza della Cisterna, another central square, which is lined with medieval homes and towers. It's the perfect spot to soak in the atmosphere and enjoy a refreshing gelato (San Gimignano is famous for its delicious gelato, after all).

While the towers are what first catch your eye, there's so much more to see and do in this charming town. Explore the narrow streets, where you'll find local artisan shops selling handmade ceramics, leather goods, and olive oil. Stop by a family-run trattoria for a taste of traditional Tuscan cuisine, or sip a glass of Vernaccia di San Gimignano, the region's famous white wine. Whether you're a history buff, a foodie, or simply someone who appreciates picturesque beauty, there's something for everyone in this delightful medieval town. San Gimignano is also a fantastic place to escape the crowds often found in more well-known Tuscan cities like Florence. Its compact size means you can easily explore it in a day, but don't be surprised if you want to linger longer. With its breathtaking views, medieval charm, and delicious local products, it's a place that invites you to slow down, take in the beauty, and fully enjoy the Tuscan experience.

Lucca

Tucked away in the heart of Tuscany, Lucca is one of those hidden gems that many travelers overlook, but once discovered, it quickly becomes unforgettable. This small yet captivating city is encircled by Renaissance-era walls that are remarkably well-preserved and still fully intact. Unlike most cities in Italy, Lucca has maintained its charm and authenticity, offering a quieter and more relaxed atmosphere compared to the bustling tourist hotspots like Florence or Pisa. With its cobbled streets, stunning piazzas, and historic architecture, Lucca feels like a secret world waiting to be explored. What makes Lucca particularly special is its city walls, which date back to the 16th century. While many cities would be defined by their monuments or famous landmarks, Lucca's walls are an attraction in themselves.

Today, the walls are a park, offering visitors a chance to walk or cycle along the tree-lined path that circles the city. Whether you're looking for a peaceful stroll or a leisurely bike ride with breathtaking views of the surrounding countryside, the city walls provide a unique perspective of Lucca's old town. It's a relaxing way to soak in the beauty of the area while getting a sense of its medieval past. As you wander through the narrow streets of Lucca's historic center, you'll discover charming boutiques, quaint cafes, and local trattorias serving authentic Tuscan dishes.

The city's heart is the Piazza dell'Anfiteatro, a stunning oval-shaped square built on the site of a Roman amphitheater. The colorful buildings that line the square are a feast for the eyes, and there's no better place to grab a coffee or enjoy a glass of wine while watching the world go by. Make sure to also visit the Torre Guinigi, a medieval tower with a quirky rooftop garden, where you can climb to the top for panoramic views of the city and beyond.

Lucca is also home to a rich cultural scene, with its impressive collection of churches, museums, and art galleries. Don't miss the Duomo di San Martino, a beautiful cathedral that's a masterpiece of Romanesque architecture, or the Museo Nazionale di Palazzo Mansi, where you can explore some of Tuscany's finest artworks. If you're in town during the summer months, Lucca hosts the Lucca Summer Festival, an annual music event that attracts big-name artists and offers a fantastic way to enjoy live performances against the backdrop of the city's historic setting.

PART 3

PISA – BEYOND THE LEANING TOWER

THE BEST OF PISA

Pisa is one of those places that surprises you. Sure, everyone comes for the Leaning Tower, snapping that classic "holding it up" photo, but there's so much more to this medieval city than just its famously tilted landmark. Beyond the tourist crowds, Pisa has a rich history, stunning architecture, and even a quirky artistic side that most visitors completely miss. If you take the time to explore, you'll find yourself wandering through charming streets, stumbling upon hidden piazzas, and even spotting street art that gives the city a modern, edgy twist.

Unlike Florence, which often steals the spotlight, Pisa moves at a slower, more relaxed pace. Its historical center is compact and easy to explore on foot, with plenty of little cafés, wine bars, and restaurants where you can grab a plate of pasta al tartufo (truffle pasta) and sip a glass of local Tuscan wine. The Arno River flows gracefully through the city, offering picturesque walking paths and the perfect backdrop for a peaceful afternoon stroll. And if you think Pisa is just a "half-day trip" destination, think again—there's plenty here to keep you entertained, whether you're a history lover, an architecture buff, or someone who just enjoys soaking in the beauty of an old Italian city.

How to Climb the Leaning Tower Without Waiting in Line

Climbing the Leaning Tower of Pisa is one of those must-do experiences that live up to the hype. The moment you step onto the spiral staircase, you'll feel the tilt—it's a little disorienting at first, but that's part of the fun! And once you reach the top, you're rewarded with stunning panoramic views of Pisa and the Tuscan countryside. But let's be real—the tower is one of the most visited landmarks in Italy, which means if you don't plan ahead, you could be stuck in a long, frustrating line.

The key to avoiding the wait is booking your ticket in advance. Many visitors make the mistake of showing up and hoping for the best, only to find that the next available climb isn't for hours. By purchasing your ticket online before you arrive, you can select your time slot and walk straight in when it's your turn. Trust me, this one small step can save you a whole lot of hassle.

Another smart move? Go early or go late. The busiest times are between 10 AM and 4 PM, when busloads of tourists from Florence pour in. If you visit first thing in the morning or closer to sunset, you'll not only avoid the biggest crowds but also get better lighting for photos—and who doesn't want a golden-hour glow for their iconic Pisa picture? And if you really want to make the most of your visit, consider exploring the Piazza dei Miracoli while you wait for your time slot. The Pisa Cathedral, Baptistery, and Camposanto are all within walking distance of the tower and offer just as much history and beauty. This way, instead of standing in line, you'll be soaking in the best of Pisa from the moment you arrive.

Piazza dei Miracoli

Let's be honest—most people rush to Pisa, snap a classic "holding up the tower" photo, and then dash off to their next destination. But here's the thing: Piazza dei Miracoli is so much more than just the Leaning Tower. It's a sprawling, stunning square filled with history, art, and hidden gems that most tourists completely overlook. If you take the time to explore beyond the famous tilt, you'll discover a place that lives up to its name—the Square of Miracles—in more ways than one.

Camposanto Monumentale

Most visitors don't even realize that Piazza dei Miracoli has a monumental cemetery tucked away behind the tower. But if you take a few extra steps, you'll find one of Pisa's most peaceful and fascinating spots. This ancient cemetery is home to Gothic arches, centuries-old tombs, and legendary frescoes, including the haunting "Triumph of Death." They say the soil here was brought back from the Holy Land, making it one of the most sacred burial grounds in Italy. It's a place where history whispers through the walls, and every stone tells a story.

The Baptistery

While the Leaning Tower steals the spotlight, the Baptistery of St. John is where the magic happens—literally. This enormous circular building isn't just the largest baptistery in Italy; it's also an acoustic wonder. Every half hour, the staff demonstrates its incredible sound quality by singing a few notes, and the building's unique dome causes the echoes to linger and harmonize all on their own. It's like hearing a ghost choir floating in the air! Step inside, stand still, and let the sound surround you—it's an experience that will stay with you long after you leave.

Everyone rushes to Pisa for that classic Leaning Tower photo, but just a few steps away, there's an experience that's even more magical—a place where the walls literally sing. That's right! The Pisa Cathedral and Baptistery aren't just architectural wonders; they hold fascinating stories and an acoustic secret that most tourists completely overlook.

Pisa Cathedral
The Pisa Cathedral is the grand beauty that often gets overshadowed by its famously tilted neighbor, but step inside, and you'll see why it deserves just as much attention. Its golden ceiling gleams in the sunlight, the massive marble

columns stretch endlessly, and intricate frescoes tell stories from centuries past. Every inch of this place is a masterpiece. But the Cathedral isn't just about stunning visuals—it's also the site of one of Galileo's greatest discoveries. Legend has it that young Galileo Galilei, sitting in church one day, noticed a chandelier swinging back and forth. As he observed, he realized the motion was perfectly timed, no matter how big or small the swing. That little moment of curiosity? It led to the discovery of pendulum motion, a principle that later influenced modern timekeeping. Who knew a church visit could change the course of science?

Now, onto the real hidden gem—the Pisa Baptistery. This isn't just the largest Baptistery in Italy; it's also home to one of the most mind-blowing acoustic effects in the world. If you're lucky enough to be inside when a staff member demonstrates, prepare for a treat. A single note sung inside this dome doesn't just echo—it harmonizes with itself, creating a hauntingly beautiful sound that lingers in the air.

This isn't some magic trick; it's all thanks to the Baptistery's unique design. The dome allows sound waves to bounce around in a way that creates natural reverb and layering effects, making it sound like the building is singing along with you. If you ever get the chance, try humming a note—you might just hear the walls respond.

Street Art in Pisa

There's a whole other side to the city that most people miss—street art. You wouldn't expect it in a place with so much history, but tucked between ancient buildings and quiet alleyways, you'll find some seriously impressive murals that tell a different story of Pisa. These aren't your typical tourist souvenirs; this art has a real edge to it, just like the city itself.

Pisa's street art scene has a little bit of everything—bold, rebellious pieces that challenge norms and thought-provoking works that can make you stop and think. It's like stumbling into a world where the modern and medieval worlds meet. Some of the most eye-catching pieces here remind you of the raw energy and creativity you'd expect from places like Berlin or New York, but they have a unique twist thanks to Pisa's historic charm.

The famous Keith Haring mural (Tuttomondo) is a must-see, sure, but there are other works that really make this city stand out. You'll find murals that aren't just about making a statement—they're about creating an experience. It's about walking down a narrow street and suddenly being hit with vivid colors or an unexpected image on the side of a crumbling wall, stopping you in your tracks. It's all part of the charm of Pisa: an ancient city with a modern pulse.

Next time you're in Pisa, take a detour and get lost in the streets. Skip the usual tourist route and let the walls of the city show you a side of Pisa that most people never see. Whether it's a splash of color or a bold statement, these murals are part of what makes Pisa so unexpectedly cool.

FOOD AND CULTURE IN PISA

There's so much more to discover in Pisa—especially when it comes to food and culture. Beyond the iconic landmarks, this charming Tuscan city boasts a rich culinary heritage, a café culture that will keep you coming back for more, and vibrant markets that capture the essence of Italian life. If you're eager to explore the tastes, traditions, and hidden gems of Pisa, here's your comprehensive guide to what to eat, where to sip, and how to soak up the authentic Tuscan culture.

What to Eat

No visit to Pisa is complete without sampling the local cuisine, and luckily for you, Pisa has a selection of unique dishes that aren't just typical Tuscan fare, but treasures in their own right. First up: Cecina. While it might sound like a strange name, this simple yet delicious dish is a must-try. Imagine a crispy, golden-brown pancake made from chickpea flour and seasoned with just a dash of olive oil and salt. Served as a snack or a light meal, Cecina is street food at its finest. Locals often grab a warm slice from a bakery, fold it in half, and enjoy it on the go. It's a humble yet flavorful experience that will quickly become a favorite.

If you're in the mood for something a little more substantial, head to a local trattoria for Pasta alla Pisana. This local twist on pasta features a rich pork ragù that's slow-cooked with tomatoes, garlic, and fresh herbs, served over perfectly al dente pasta. It's hearty, comforting, and the ultimate representation of Pisa's rustic, no-frills culinary style. Another dish you shouldn't miss is Ribollita—a traditional Tuscan soup made from leftover bread, beans, and seasonal vegetables like kale. This humble dish has been passed down for generations and offers a true taste of the Tuscan countryside.

For dessert, you can't leave without trying Torta co' Bischeri. This Pisan pastry is made from rich chocolate, candied fruits, and nuts, all enclosed in a flaky crust. It's the perfect treat to end a meal, or if you're like many locals, you'll pick one up to enjoy alongside your afternoon espresso. It's not as widely known outside of Pisa, making it an even sweeter find for those willing to venture into the city's bakeries.

Best Coffee Shops and Aperitivo Spots
No matter where you are in Italy, coffee is always a serious affair—and Pisa is no exception. Start your day with a morning espresso at Caffè dei Neri, an unassuming yet charming café located in the heart of Pisa's historic center. With its cozy, vintage ambiance and a local clientele, it's the perfect place to people-watch and enjoy a shot of rich, flavorful espresso. The café's simplicity and focus on quality make it a favorite among those who appreciate a truly authentic coffee experience.

If you're in the mood for something a little more indulgent, Caffè Delle Logge is the spot for you. This upscale café offers not only delicious cappuccinos but also an extensive selection of pastries, perfect for an afternoon pick-me-up. Located in a quieter area of the city, it's a great place to relax and enjoy your coffee while flipping through a book or simply enjoying the peaceful surroundings. As for its design, think vintage Italian charm, with plush seating and large windows letting in tons of natural light.

In the evening, aperitivo culture comes alive in Pisa, and one of the best spots to enjoy it is at Osteria di Caffè del Borgo. Aperitivo is Italy's answer to happy hour, a time for locals to unwind with an aperitif and small bites before dinner. Here, you'll find a selection of local wines, cocktails, and classic Italian appetizers like bruschetta, olives, and cheese platters.

The energy is laid-back but lively, and it's a great way to engage with the local culture while sipping on a refreshing negroni or a glass of Chianti.

Local Markets And Hidden Shopping Gems

For those who want to experience the authentic heart of Pisa, markets are the best place to start. The Mercato di San Michele is one of the city's oldest and most beloved markets, and it's the perfect place to shop for fresh produce, local meats, cheeses, and olive oil. This bustling open-air market has been a meeting place for locals for centuries, and it's still as vibrant as ever. Whether you're picking up a few ingredients to cook your own meal or simply browsing the stalls to see what's in season, the market is a great spot to soak up the local atmosphere.

For a more off-the-beaten-path shopping experience, head to Borgo Stretto, one of Pisa's most picturesque shopping streets. This narrow, medieval lane is lined with independent boutiques offering everything from handmade leather goods and artisan jewelry to local crafts and stylish clothing. Here, you'll get a sense of the true character of Pisa's artisans and shop owners, who are eager to share their creations and stories with visitors. After wandering the streets and picking up a few unique pieces, stop for a quick coffee or gelato at one of the quaint cafes along the way.

Pisa also has its share of antique shops for those with a love for history. If you're an antiques enthusiast, take a stroll through the city's charming corners and discover everything from antique books and vintage maps to rare porcelain and old coins. These shops are often tucked away in little alleys or hidden inside historic buildings, making it feel like you're uncovering a piece of Pisa's past with every new find. Plus, you'll find that many of the owners are more than happy to share their knowledge of the items, making your visit a true learning experience.

The beauty of Pisa isn't just in its history, art, and architecture—it's also in its food and culture, which are deeply intertwined. From the simple flavors of a local soup to the rich wines shared at aperitivo time, food is a reflection of the city's long history and the daily lives of its residents. As you experience Pisa's unique culinary scene, you'll also be embracing its cultural richness—a city that values both tradition and innovation, all served on a plate. This combination of food and culture is what makes Pisa not just a place to visit, but a place to truly immerse yourself in. So, take your time, savor every bite, and get ready to discover the authentic heart of this Tuscan gem.

BORGO STRETTO

SCAN THE QR CODE

HOW TO SCAN THE QR CODE

To access the content of the QR code (Google map)

On a smartphone:

1. Open your camera app.
2. Point it at the QR code.
3. Tap the notification or link that pops up on the screen.

If your camera doesn't support QR scanning, download a free QR code scanner app from your app store

THE BEST PHOTO SPOTS IN PISA

Pisa is a city filled with hidden corners, stunning vistas, and architectural gems that make for incredible photographs. Beyond the tourist-heavy spots, there are peaceful locations where you can catch the city at its best — bathed in golden hour light, sparkling in the stillness of dawn, or quiet under the warm Tuscan sun. If you want to capture the authentic essence of Pisa, there's no shortage of spots that offer everything from charming streets and lush gardens to picturesque riverside views. Whether you're an aspiring photographer or just someone who loves snapping the perfect shot, Pisa has some unforgettable photo opportunities waiting to be explored.

The Secret Viewpoint Most Tourists Miss

Piazza dei Cavalieri
You've probably heard about the crowded landmarks around Pisa, but there's one spot that is often overlooked by the typical tourist crowd — Piazza dei Cavalieri. This square, located a short walk from the more famous areas, is a hidden gem that lets you capture Pisa in its quieter, academic glory. Home to the Palazzo della Carovana and the Scuola Normale Superiore, this square is brimming with history and impressive architecture. The majestic buildings, with their intricate facades, evoke a sense of grandeur and are perfect for photography, especially when the sun casts dramatic shadows along the stone walls.

In the early morning or later in the afternoon, the light in Piazza dei Cavalieri is magical. The golden hues of the sun gently illuminate the historic buildings, and the tranquility of the square gives it an almost cinematic feel. Here, you'll have the chance to take photos of Pisa that most visitors don't see, capturing the city's rich cultural heritage without the crowds. The piazza's charm lies in its timeless beauty, making it an ideal spot for those seeking a more authentic and off-the-beaten-path image of Pisa.

Along the Arno River
Pisa's Arno River runs through the heart of the city, and its banks provide some of the most picturesque and serene photo spots. While the river itself is a central feature, it's the sunset

views that make it truly special. One of the best places to capture the sunset is Ponte di Mezzo, a bridge that spans the Arno and offers sweeping views of the river and Pisa's skyline. As the sun dips below the horizon, the colors of the sky and the reflections on the water create a breathtaking scene that you won't want to miss. The light during the golden hour enhances the beauty of the historic buildings along the riverbanks, making your photographs feel like they're straight out of a dream.

What makes this spot unique is the peaceful atmosphere — many visitors don't venture too far from the Leaning Tower, leaving this area more tranquil for those who do. If you're after more intimate shots, take a walk along the river and discover hidden pockets along the banks. You might come across old benches where locals sit and chat, the soft ripples of the river, and narrow alleyways that offer great views of the city from a different angle. These hidden corners add depth to your photographs, showcasing the quieter side of Pisa away from the crowds.

Borgo Stretto
For those who love to capture street scenes and the vibrant life of a city, Borgo Stretto should be on your list. This picturesque, pedestrian-only street is one of Pisa's most charming places to stroll, with its narrow lanes, vibrant storefronts, and beautifully preserved medieval architecture. The streets are lined with colorful buildings and arched passageways, making it an ideal spot for photography, especially if you want to capture the essence of everyday Pisa. The play of light and shadows, with the sun peeking through

the arches and illuminating the shop windows, creates the perfect setting for an authentic city scene.

In the mornings, Borgo Stretto is quieter, offering a chance to snap the street without the hustle and bustle of midday crowds. The cafes here are perfect for people-watching, and you'll often see locals stopping for their espresso or chatting with shop owners. As you walk down the street, you'll come across many small boutiques, artisan shops, and local galleries that add a distinct charm to the area. Whether you're capturing the bustling energy of a busy street or simply the quaint beauty of a forgotten corner, Borgo Stretto offers a plethora of photo opportunities that will make your collection of Pisa shots stand out.

Orto Botanico
Pisa's Orto Botanico (Botanical Garden) is another hidden gem that is often overlooked by tourists but offers a stunning backdrop for nature photography. Located just a short distance from the main attractions, this lush garden is home to centuries-old trees, winding paths, and vibrant flowerbeds. As one of the oldest botanical gardens in Europe, it's not just a peaceful escape from the hustle and bustle of the city; it's also a place filled with beauty, perfect for capturing those natural, organic shots.

Whether you're focusing on the delicate petals of flowers, the intricate details of ancient trees, or the serene pathways that lead through the garden, Orto Botanico offers plenty of opportunities to get creative with your photos. The garden's design allows you to frame shots of hidden corners where light filters through the trees, creating soft, dreamy images. It's also an excellent spot for capturing macro photos of plants or even portraits with the tranquil garden setting as your backdrop. For those looking to escape the crowds and find a peaceful, green oasis, this garden is the perfect place to snap some quiet, contemplative shots.

The Arno River at Dusk
Finally, if you're seeking the perfect photo of Pisa at dusk, Ponte di Mezzo provides a stunning view of the city as the last light of day fades. The buildings along the river become beautifully silhouetted against the changing sky, creating an almost magical atmosphere. The Arno River reflects the colors of the sunset, making it an ideal location to capture a unique, romantic photo of the city.

As the city begins to settle down, you can take photos of the riverside, the bridges, and the buildings that line the banks, all bathed in a soft glow. It's the perfect spot for capturing the city's calm and serene side after the excitement of the day.

In the end, Pisa has a wealth of photogenic spots that go beyond the typical tourist imagery. So, pack your camera, explore these spots, and see a side of Pisa that's just waiting to be discovered.

PART 4

PRACTICAL TIPS AND LOCAL EXPERIENCES

INSIDER TIPS FOR THE BEST EXPERIENCE IN PISA AND FLORENCE

When it comes to Florence and Pisa, there's a lot more to these stunning cities than the classic tourist trail. You might know about the Leaning Tower and the Duomo, but there's a whole world of local secrets, hidden gems, and insider knowledge waiting to make your experience richer, smoother, and just a little more magical. Whether you're looking to avoid the crowds, get the best bang for your buck, or dive deep into the cultural heart of Tuscany, these insider tips will help you see both cities like a local. And who doesn't love a good insider secret?

How to Skip the Lines And Avoid Tourist Traps

Let's face it — no one likes waiting in long lines, especially when you've got so much to see and do in a city as beautiful as Florence or Pisa. Luckily, there are a few clever hacks that'll save you time and energy, leaving you with more hours to explore and less time spent standing around.

1. **Buy Skip-the-Line Tickets**: This one's a no-brainer! For popular attractions like the Uffizi Gallery in Florence or the Leaning Tower of Pisa, booking a skip-the-line ticket can make all the difference. You'll pay a little more, but the extra cost is worth it. You'll breeze right past those lines that can stretch for hours, especially during peak tourist seasons. Plus, many attractions now offer timed entry, meaning you pick a specific time to enter, so you don't waste any time.

2. **Get Early or Late**: If you're looking to beat the crowds, consider visiting major sites at opening time or just before closing. The Uffizi Gallery and Piazza dei Miracoli are significantly less crowded during the first hour after opening, and you'll have more space to appreciate the art or architecture without bumping into a dozen selfie sticks. In Florence, go early for the Duomo, and for Pisa, visit the Leaning Tower during late afternoon when the light is stunning and the crowds have started to thin out.

3. **Stay in Lesser-Known Areas**: Instead of staying directly in the heart of Florence or Pisa, why not consider staying in neighborhoods like Oltrarno in Florence or the quieter

districts in Pisa? They give you access to the main sights without the constant crowds and tourist traps. Plus, you'll be supporting local businesses while getting a more authentic experience.

4. **Book Tours in Advance**: If you want to skip long waits and gain deeper insight, many tours offer fast-track entry. Walking tours or guided visits often come with skip-the-line perks, so do some research and book in advance to avoid wasting valuable time.

Budget Travel Tips vs. Luxury Experiences

Whether you're traveling on a shoestring budget or you've got a bit more to splurge on your trip, Pisa and Florence have something for everyone. Let's break down the best ways to enjoy both cities no matter your budget.

Budget-Friendly Travel Tips
1. **Walk or Bike Everywhere**: Both Florence and Pisa are incredibly walkable, and getting around on foot will not only save you money on transportation but also give you a chance to stumble upon hidden gems that aren't on any map. Rent a bike for a day, especially in Florence's Oltrarno District or along the Arno River for a peaceful, scenic way to explore the city. It's a great way to see the city like a local, and it's much cheaper than taking taxis or buses.

2. **Free Attractions**: Florence and Pisa have tons of free attractions to enjoy. Wander around Piazza della Signoria in Florence, where you can marvel at replicas of famous statues like David (originals are in the Accademia). In Pisa, take a stroll along the Arno River or visit the Botanical Gardens — both are free and perfect for a relaxing afternoon. The Piazza dei Miracoli itself is stunning to view from the outside, even if you don't climb the Leaning Tower.

3. **Cheap Eats**: Florence's Mercato Centrale offers delicious local food at reasonable prices. You can enjoy fresh pasta, cheese, cured meats, and pizza, all served by local vendors. In Pisa, check out the small trattorias where the locals eat. Try Pasta al Pomodoro, a simple yet delicious meal, at budget-friendly prices in places like Osteria dei Cavalieri or Trattoria Da Bruno. The best part? You can always grab a quick bite of gelato afterward for just a couple of euros.

Luxury Experiences
1. **Private Wine Tasting Tours**: If you want to indulge, Tuscany's wine country is a must. Book a private wine tour in the Chianti region. Many tours can be customized to include vineyard visits, private wine tastings, and gourmet meals in Tuscan estates. Imagine sipping on world-class wines, paired with the freshest local food, while surrounded by rolling vineyards and cypress trees — it's the epitome of luxury travel in Tuscany.

2. **Stay at Boutique Hotels or Luxury Resorts**: Florence and Pisa both have their fair share of charming boutique hotels and top-tier luxury resorts. If you want a touch of elegance

and historical charm, consider staying at Hotel Brunelleschi in Florence, which is set inside a former church and medieval tower. For a true Tuscan countryside escape, check out Belmond Castello di Casole in the rolling hills of Chianti for a stunning experience.

3. **Private Art Tours And Exclusive Access**: For art lovers, exclusive, private guided tours of the Uffizi Gallery or Pitti Palace give you deeper insight into masterpieces and allow you to skip the crowds. Some tours even offer behind-the-scenes access, so you can explore areas that regular visitors don't have access to.

Local Festivals and Events Happening in 2025

Both Florence and Pisa are brimming with culture, and 2025 is packed with exciting local festivals, events, and celebrations that you'll want to experience. Here are a few of the must-see events happening during your visit:

1. **Pisa's Luminara (June 16, 2025)**: One of the most magical events in Pisa is Luminara, which takes place every June. During this festival, the city's landmarks, including the Pisa Cathedral, are lit by thousands of candles, creating a breathtaking scene. It's a festival of lights that draws both locals and tourists alike, and you'll want to capture these beautiful, glowing moments.

2. **Florence's Pitti Immagine Uomo (January 2025)**: For fashion enthusiasts, Florence is home to one of the world's leading fashion events, Pitti Immagine Uomo. This exclusive fashion week brings together top designers, brands, and influencers, and if you're lucky enough to be in town during this event, it's a chance to witness the cutting edge of men's fashion and the city's chicest crowds.

3. **Florence's Festa della Rificolona (September 7, 2025)**: This ancient festival celebrates the eve of the Nativity of the Virgin Mary with a parade of lanterns and candles, as people march through the streets in traditional costumes. The festival is full of music, food, and fun, making it an unforgettable experience for those visiting Florence in the fall.

Whether you're in Pisa or Florence, both cities come alive with vibrant culture, stunning experiences, and festivals that will leave you with memories for a lifetime. With these insider tips, you'll avoid the typical tourist traps and instead enjoy these beautiful cities like a true local.

WHERE TO STAY

When it comes to choosing where to stay in Florence and Pisa, the options are as diverse as the cities themselves. From the bustling historic centers to quiet, more local areas, there's a place for every type of traveler. If you're looking to be in the heart of the action or prefer to escape to a peaceful corner of Tuscany, the following guide will help you make the right choice for a memorable stay.

Top Neighborhoods in Florence

Florence is a city where art, history, and culture come together, and where you choose to stay can truly shape your experience. The historic center, where the majority of Florence's famous landmarks are located, offers a bustling atmosphere with endless opportunities to explore. But if you're after something a little quieter or more local, the city has plenty of hidden gems to offer.

1. **Centro Storico (Historic Center)**: This is the heart of Florence, and staying here means you're just a stone's throw away from iconic sights like the Duomo, Uffizi Gallery, Piazza della Signoria, and the Ponte Vecchio. The streets are lined with charming boutiques, cafes, and trattorias, making it an ideal area for those who want to soak up the city's vibrant energy. Some of the best hotels here include Hotel Savoy, which blends classic luxury with modern flair, and Hotel L'Orologio, perfect for those who love sophisticated design. Keep in mind, the area can get a bit crowded, especially in peak seasons, but for many, this is the true Florence experience.

2. **Oltrarno**: If you're looking to avoid the heavy tourist crowds but still be close to all the action, Oltrarno is the neighborhood for you. Located just across the Arno River, this district is filled with local artisans, independent boutiques, and traditional Tuscan restaurants. Here, you'll find quieter streets, intimate cafes, and the beautiful Piazza Santo Spirito, where you can unwind like a local. Hotels like Hotel Pitti Palace al Ponte Vecchio offer easy access to both the iconic sites on the other side of the river and the laid-back vibe of Oltrarno. The area also has a great nightlife scene, especially around Piazza della Passera, where you can enjoy a drink at a cozy wine bar.

3. **Santa Croce**: For a mix of art, history, and authenticity, Santa Croce offers a fantastic location. It's home to the

famous Basilica di Santa Croce, where you can pay homage to greats like Michelangelo and Galileo. This area is less touristy than the historic center but still offers easy access to Florence's top attractions. B&B Santa Croce is a charming and affordable option in this area, giving you a cozy, local feel without sacrificing comfort. The neighborhood also offers some of Florence's best gelato and pizza spots, so you can eat like a true Florentine.

Best Places to Stay in Pisa

Pisa is a smaller city than Florence, but choosing the right neighborhood can still make a big difference in your experience. While many visitors flock to the area around the Leaning Tower of Pisa, there are other neighborhoods that offer a more relaxed and authentic slice of life in the city.

1. **Near the Leaning Tower (Piazza dei Miracoli)**: Staying near the Leaning Tower means you're just minutes away from one of the most famous landmarks in the world. While it's convenient for first-time visitors, be prepared for crowds, especially in high season. Hotels like Hotel Pisa Tower and Grand Hotel Duomo are right near the tower and offer great views, though they can be a bit pricier than other options. You'll also have easy access to restaurants and cafes catering to tourists, which might not always offer the best local cuisine.

2. **San Francesco**: For a more authentic, local vibe, consider staying in San Francesco, which is just a short walk from the Piazza dei Miracoli but offers a more residential, relaxed atmosphere. It's perfect for those who want to avoid the crowds near the tower but still be close to the action. In this area, you'll find charming streets lined with traditional restaurants, local shops, and beautiful parks. Hotels like Hotel Di Stefano are located here and offer a quiet retreat while still being close to the major attractions.

3. **Città Giardino**: A hidden gem for those who prefer a peaceful escape, Città Giardino is a residential area with leafy streets and a more local feel. It's located a little further from the main tourist attractions, but it's worth the stay for those looking for a more tranquil Pisa experience. The area is filled with parks, cafes, and great local eateries. You can stay at places like Villa Tower Inn, which is known for its beautiful gardens and serene environment, offering a relaxing retreat after a day of sightseeing.

Luxury vs. Budget Options in Both Cities

Whether you're looking to indulge in luxury or save a bit on accommodation, both Florence and Pisa offer a variety of options to suit all budgets. Here's a breakdown of what you can expect from luxury and budget stays in both cities.

Luxury Options
1. **Florence**: For a truly luxurious experience, Florence has no shortage of opulent hotels. The St. Regis Florence is a grand 5-star hotel located on the banks of the Arno River, offering spectacular views, fine dining, and impeccable service. Four Seasons Hotel Firenze is another standout, with its gorgeous gardens and world-class amenities. If you want to feel like royalty, consider staying in Palazzo Vecchietti, a historical palace turned luxury hotel, right near the Duomo. Florence's luxury hotels are often housed in beautiful Renaissance palaces or villas, and they offer the perfect base for those seeking an exclusive experience.

2. **Pisa**: Though smaller than Florence, Pisa also offers some high-end accommodations. The Grand Hotel Duomo is a fantastic choice if you want to stay near the Leaning Tower, with its elegant interiors and rooftop views. For something more secluded and romantic, Villa Tower Inn provides a tranquil, luxurious setting just outside the main tourist areas. The charm of these luxury hotels lies in their intimate settings, beautiful surroundings, and top-notch service.

Budget Options
1. **Florence**: If you're traveling on a budget but still want to experience the beauty of Florence, there are plenty of great affordable options. Hotel Delle Nazioni offers comfortable, budget-friendly rooms just a short walk from the train station, making it a perfect base for sightseeing. B&B La Dimora degli Angeli is another great option for those looking for an affordable stay in the historic center. For a more unique experience, consider booking a Florentine apartment through platforms like Airbnb. It'll give you the flexibility to cook your meals and live like a local.

2. **Pisa**: Pisa's budget accommodations are equally plentiful. Hotel Francesco is an affordable yet comfortable choice just a 10-minute walk from the Leaning Tower. It's perfect for those who want to stay close to the action without breaking the bank. If you're looking for a more unique, homely feel, consider staying at The Arno Guest House in the San Francisco area. It's an affordable guesthouse that offers clean, simple rooms and a great location.

Stay central if you want the full tourist experience, or head to quieter neighborhoods if you want to experience these cities like a local. Whichever option you choose, you'll be sure to enjoy the charm, culture, and beauty that these two iconic cities have to offer.

TRAVEL CHECKLIST

Whether you're embarking on your first adventure to these iconic Italian cities or returning for another round of pasta, art, and history, this checklist will ensure you're fully prepared to make the most of your time in Florence and Pisa. From packing tips to must-try experiences, we've got you covered.

Packing Essentials

1. Comfortable Walking Shoes

Both Florence and Pisa are best explored on foot, and many of the streets are cobbled, so comfortable shoes are a must! Opt for sturdy yet stylish shoes that can handle hours of walking.

2. Light Layers and a Light Jacket

The weather in Tuscany can be unpredictable. Be prepared for a mix of sunshine, possible rain, and cooler evenings, especially in spring and fall. Pack light layers that you can easily take off or add on as needed.

3. Sunscreen And Sunglasses

Tuscany's sun can be intense, especially during summer, so protect yourself with sunscreen and sunglasses. You'll be outdoors a lot—whether you're wandering the piazzas or taking in the views from Piazzale Michelangelo.

4. A Camera (or Smartphone)

You won't want to miss capturing all the beauty that Florence and Pisa have to offer. Whether it's the grand Duomo in Florence or the Leaning Tower in Pisa, there are countless photo opportunities waiting for you.

5. Travel Adapter

Italy uses a type C or F plug, so don't forget to pack a travel adapter if you're coming from abroad. You don't want to miss the chance to charge your devices after all that sightseeing!

6. A Light Backpack or Crossbody Bag

A small bag is perfect for keeping your essentials (wallet, camera, sunscreen) close while you explore. Avoid heavy backpacks or tote bags as they might get in the way while navigating through narrow streets or in crowded spots.

7. A Reusable Water Bottle

Florence and Pisa have plenty of public drinking fountains, where you can fill up your bottle with fresh, cool water. Save money and stay hydrated while you explore.

Must-Have Travel Apps

1. Google Maps

While walking through the historic streets of Florence and Pisa, having a reliable map app is essential. Google Maps can help you navigate to key attractions, restaurants, and hidden gems, especially when you're wandering off the beaten path.

2. The Florence And Pisa Official Tourist Apps

Both cities have apps with detailed information about museums, events, and tips for getting around. They're great tools for planning your days in each city.

3. Duolingo or Google Translate

While most people in Florence and Pisa speak English, it's always helpful (and fun!) to know a few words in Italian. Duolingo or Google Translate will help you with phrases like "Where is the bathroom?" or "How much does this cost?"

4. The Fork (La Forchetta)

This app lets you reserve a table at top restaurants and often offers discounts and exclusive deals. It's a great tool for securing a seat at popular places without the stress of waiting in line.

Florence And Pisa Experience Checklist

1. Climb the Leaning Tower of Pisa

Yes, you have to do it! The iconic Leaning Tower is a must-see and a must-climb. But don't forget to book your tickets in advance so you can avoid long lines.

2. Explore the Uffizi Gallery in Florence

Home to some of the most renowned masterpieces in the world, the Uffizi Gallery should be at the top of your Florence itinerary. Take your time with works by Botticelli, Michelangelo, and da Vinci.

3. Stroll along the Arno River

Florence's Ponte Vecchio and the view of the city from the river's edge are breathtaking. Take a leisurely stroll or hop on a boat for a different perspective.

4. Indulge in Tuscan Cuisine

You can't visit Florence and Pisa without eating like a local! Make sure to try bistecca alla Fiorentina (Florentine steak) and sample local wines. Don't forget to stop by a gelateria for authentic gelato.

5. Admire the View from Piazzale Michelangelo

This is the best spot for panoramic views of Florence, especially at sunset. It's a great spot to take in the city's stunning architecture, including the Duomo and Ponte Vecchio.

6. Visit the Pisa Cathedral and Baptistery
Most tourists rush to the Leaning Tower, but don't miss the opportunity to step inside the beautiful Pisa Cathedral and discover the Baptistery's famous acoustic phenomenon. You'll be amazed at how the sound changes when you stand in certain spots!

7. Check out the Street Art in Pisa
Pisa may be known for its historic sites, but the city also has a thriving street art scene. Take a stroll through the streets and you'll come across murals and installations that reflect the city's contemporary culture.

8. Wander through the Boboli Gardens in Florence
Escape the city's hustle and bustle by spending time in the lush Boboli Gardens. This Renaissance garden offers stunning views of Florence and is the perfect spot for a relaxing afternoon.

9. Take a Day Trip to the Chianti Wine Region
Don't miss the chance to explore Tuscany's wine country. Whether you book a guided tour or venture on your own, visiting the vineyards and tasting the local wines is an experience you won't forget.

Pro Tip
Avoid the tourist traps by steering clear of the restaurants directly next to major attractions like the Leaning Tower of Pisa. Instead, wander a few streets away to find authentic, local places with better food and prices. Locals

tend to head to hidden spots where the food is fresh and the ambiance is relaxed.

With this checklist in hand, you're all set for an unforgettable adventure in Florence and Pisa. Safe travels and enjoy the beauty and charm of these two stunning Italian cities.

Travel Checklist

DATE: _____
DESTINATION: _____

CLOTHES
- [ ] _____
- [ ] _____
- [ ] _____
- [ ] _____
- [ ] _____
- [ ] _____
- [ ] _____
- [ ] _____
- [ ] _____
- [ ] _____
- [ ] _____
- [ ] _____

BASICS
- [ ] _____
- [ ] _____
- [ ] _____
- [ ] _____
- [ ] _____

SHOES
- [ ] _____
- [ ] _____
- [ ] _____
- [ ] _____
- [ ] _____

TOILETRIES
- [ ] _____
- [ ] _____
- [ ] _____
- [ ] _____
- [ ] _____
- [ ] _____
- [ ] _____
- [ ] _____

ELECTRONICS
- [ ] _____
- [ ] _____
- [ ] _____
- [ ] _____
- [ ] _____
- [ ] _____

ACCESSORIES
- [ ] _____
- [ ] _____
- [ ] _____
- [ ] _____
- [ ] _____
- [ ] _____
- [ ] _____

OTHER
- [ ] _____
- [ ] _____
- [ ] _____

IMPORTANT
- [ ] _____
- [ ] _____
- [ ] _____
- [ ] _____

Travel Checklist

DATE: _____
DESTINATION: _____

CLOTHES
- [ ] _____
- [ ] _____
- [ ] _____
- [ ] _____
- [ ] _____
- [ ] _____
- [ ] _____
- [ ] _____
- [ ] _____
- [ ] _____
- [ ] _____
- [ ] _____

BASICS
- [ ] _____
- [ ] _____
- [ ] _____
- [ ] _____
- [ ] _____
- [ ] _____

SHOES
- [ ] _____
- [ ] _____
- [ ] _____
- [ ] _____
- [ ] _____

TOILETRIES
- [ ] _____
- [ ] _____
- [ ] _____
- [ ] _____
- [ ] _____
- [ ] _____
- [ ] _____
- [ ] _____

ELECTRONICS
- [ ] _____
- [ ] _____
- [ ] _____
- [ ] _____
- [ ] _____
- [ ] _____
- [ ] _____

ACCESSORIES
- [ ] _____
- [ ] _____
- [ ] _____
- [ ] _____
- [ ] _____
- [ ] _____
- [ ] _____
- [ ] _____

OTHER
- [ ] _____
- [ ] _____
- [ ] _____

Important
- [ ] _____
- [ ] _____
- [ ] _____
- [ ] _____

CONCLUSION

If you've made it to the end of this Florence and Pisa Travel Guide 2025, thank you—truly. Writing this book felt like planning a dream trip with a good friend, and I hope it's felt that way for you too.

By now, you've probably built a vivid picture in your mind of cobbled streets winding through Renaissance art and sun-drenched piazzas, the aroma of fresh pasta wafting from tiny trattorias, and the unmistakable charm of two cities that have captured hearts for centuries. From iconic spots like the Duomo and the Leaning Tower to those little hidden corners only locals know about, this guide was created to help you explore more deeply, wander more freely, and experience Italy not just as a tourist—but as a curious soul in love with discovery.

I hope you feel more prepared and a little more inspired. Whether you're off for a romantic getaway, a solo adventure, or a food-filled escape with friends, my wish is that your trip to Florence and Pisa brings you joy, wonder, and memories you'll hold onto for years.

And hey—if this book helped you in any way, I'd be incredibly grateful if you left a review on Amazon. It doesn't have to be long—just a few honest words about what you found helpful or enjoyable. It helps other travelers find the book, and it means the world to indie authors like me who pour heart and soul into creating something useful.

Wishing you safe travels, magical moments, and maybe a little more gelato than you planned on.

Arrivederci,
And buon viaggio!

TRAVEL PLANNER

"IT'S OKAY TO TAKE A BREAK."

DESTINATION: DURATION:

MUST VISIT PLACES
-
-
-
-

FOODS TO TRY

_____
_____
_____
_____

DAY 1	DAY 2	DAY 3

BUDGET

NOTE

_____
_____
_____

TRAVEL PLANNER

"IT'S OKAY TO TAKE A BREAK."

DESTINATION: _____ DURATION: _____

MUST VISIT PLACES
-
-
-
-

FOODS TO TRY
_____
_____
_____
_____

DAY 1

DAY 2

DAY 3

BUDGET

NOTE
_____
_____
_____
_____

TRAVEL PLANNER

"IT'S OKAY TO TAKE A BREAK."

DESTINATION: DURATION:

MUST VISIT PLACES
-
-
-
-

FOODS TO TRY

DAY 1

DAY 2

DAY 3

BUDGET

NOTE

Printed in Great Britain
by Amazon